D0916876

THE
SCARLET CORD

Nothing but the Blood of Jesus

"I have just finished reading *The Scarlet Cord: Nothing but the Blood of Jesus.* This powerful book has put a fresh fire in my heart for world evangelization. To those serious about world missions, I recommend this book strongly, and to those not serious about world missions, I recommend it even more."

—*Timothy Johnson*, Dominican Republic: foreign-based missionary for over 25 years

THE SCARLET CORD

Nothing but the Blood of Jesus

A CONCISE CALL TO WORLD MISSIONS

JON & ANN DUNAGAN

http://harvestministry.org

The Scarlet Cord: Nothing but the Blood of Jesus
ISBN 978-0-9832505-6-2

Cover Design by Caela Rose Buchholtz

Toll Free: 1-866-260-9563

Library of Congress Cataloging-in-Publication Data

Dunagan, Jon. Dunagan, Ann. The Scarlet Cord: Nothing
but the Blood of Jesus / Jon & Ann Dunagan. Includes
bibliographical references. ISBN 978-0-9832505-6-2 (pbk. :
alk. paper) 1. Christian
theology. 2. Missions-Study and teaching. 1. Title.

Printed in Canada

This book is dedicated to our Lord and Savior,
JESUS CHRIST

. . . and for all those for whom He shed
His precious blood
who have yet to hear of His sacrifice.

**Never pity
missionaries;
envy them.**

**They are where the
real action is-
where life and death,
sin and grace,
Heaven and Hell
converge.**

—Robert C. Shannon

Preface

This is a missions book.

It's a call for you to accept God's great challenge—to rise above the norm of a typical and ordinary Christian life, and to join Him in a great adventure. It's a call to obey God's Great Commission—and to make your life count, for eternity.

But be forewarned. Completely following Jesus Christ will not always be easy, or comfortable. The tough subjects addressed in this book—such as taking up your cross and going to the nations, or pondering the eternal condition of "lost souls"—are not popular themes. Many Christians would rather focus on how to be happy.

Let's be honest here. It's typical and normal to want an easy life and pleasant things.

Most people would prefer a delicious feast, rather than an extended fast. Most people would prefer to stay at a fabulous hotel, rather than in a filthy mud hut.

And perhaps our Lord Jesus might have preferred reigning from His heavenly throne . . . more than His suffering on the cross.

Yet the Bible describes "a joy" set before Jesus as He surrendered to the will and love of His heavenly Father, despite the cost. And empowered by His grace, we too can do whatever God wants, and enjoy the adventure!

God does want to bless us, but His greatest rewards are more satisfying than any temporal or earthly pleasure, and His heavenly crowns surpass anything our world can offer. As Christians, we are already blessed, even more than we realize, especially with God's gift of salvation. But we are blessed to be a blessing to others!

His desire is for us to get out of our comfort-zones of selfishness and ease—and with "a joy" set before us, to take up our cross, and to follow Him. As we grow in our relationship with God, we will desire more of His love. As God's love develops in our hearts, we will want to join His mission. Our prayer is for this book to spark that interest, and more.

Jesus Christ allowed His hands and feet to be "pierced" by Roman nails. As His blood flowed down that rugged cross, it was God's love that was poured out for you and for this world. As we were writing this little book, we prayed for those of you who would someday read these pages, and as we prayed, that word "pierced" kept coming to our minds.

Our Lord was pierced because of God's perfect love. As you take hold of *The Scarlet Cord: Nothing but the Blood of Jesus,* may God's passion pierce your heart.

Jon & Ann Dunagan
Harvest Ministry — Mission-Minded Families

A Passion for Souls

Give me a passion for souls, dear Lord,
A passion to save the lost;
O that Thy love were by all adored,
And welcomed at any cost.

Jesus, I long, I long to be winning,
Men who are lost, and constantly sinning;
O may this hour become of beginning
The story of pardon to tell . . .

How shall this passion for souls be mine?
Lord, make Thou the answer clear;
Help me to throw out the old life line
To those who are struggling near.

—Herbert G. Tovey, 1888

**Why should anyone
hear the Gospel twice,
before everyone
has heard it once?**

—Oswald J. Smith,
Missionary Evangelist

Contents

What can wash away
my sin?

Nothing but the blood
of Jesus.

What can make me
whole again?

Nothing but the blood
of Jesus.

—Robert Lowry

1

Saved to the Uttermost
The Symbolism of Rahab's Scarlet Cord

> "...you were without Christ, being aliens from
> the commonwealth of Israel and strangers
> from the covenants of promise, having no hope
> and without God in the world. But now in
> Christ Jesus you who once were far off have been brought
> near by the blood of Christ."
>
> —Ephesians 2:12-13

In the Old Testament account of Joshua and the battle of Jericho, the scene is one of devastation and death; yet in the midst of judgment on a wicked city and victory for the people of Israel, the Bible turns our attention to God's mercy and forgiveness . . . and a simple scarlet cord.

By faith, a prostitute named Rahab believes in God. By faith, this Gentile woman hides two Israelite spies, and in obedience to their specific instructions, she extends a scarlet cord through her window on the wall. And by faith, she is saved from destruction.

The title of this book, *The Scarlet Cord*, is taken from this Bible story of Rahab (from Joshua, chapters 2 and 6).

It wasn't just a coincidence that the color of Rahab's cord was red. This "scarlet cord" is an important symbol, intertwined throughout the entire Word of God. It is

7

a foreshadow of God's payment for sin, emphasizing His required blood sacrifice. Ultimately, the scarlet cord represents the blood of our Lord Jesus, "the Lamb slain from the foundation of the world" (Revelation 13:8).

The scarlet cord is a biblical object lesson of God's passionate mercy and His amazing grace!

Perhaps no other Bible story so dramatically shares the power of the blood. Prior to meeting God's people—and symbolically, before Rahab "applied the blood" to her life by trusting in God and letting down the scarlet cord—her life was hopeless.

As a prostitute, Rahab had likely encountered abuse, disease, disgrace, and scorn. In moral character, Rahab was a deceiver, a liar to the king of Jericho, and a traitor to her own people (not exactly the type of woman you would want your son to marry).

The scarlet cord is a biblical object lesson of God's amazing grace!

Yet the Bible says, "the LORD does not see as man sees; for man looks at the outward appearance, but the LORD looks at the heart" (I Samuel 16:7).

Regardless of her wretched past, Rahab put her trust in God and her faith pleased Him. She begged for the spies to give her a "true token" to symbolize God's promise for her safety. In response, the spies instructed her to let down a scarlet cord, with reference to her life being spared by its covering. Thus, by trusting in the saving promise represented by that scarlet cord, Rahab also "symbolically" placed her trust in God's future Messiah and Savior, Jesus Christ.

Like the example of Abraham in the Old Testament, who ". . . believed in the LORD" and it was "accounted" for righteousness (Genesis 15:6), Rahab's faith was credited to her spiritual account. Centuries later, on the cross of Calvary, Jesus Christ paid her debt in full.

But that's not all. Because of Rahab's faith, God responded by also saving everyone who believed in her message of God's hope. All who joined with her—under that scarlet cord—were saved from death, including her father, mother, sisters, brothers, and all who were crowded into her home. When God saves, He really saves!

Symbolizing the Blood of Jesus

The Bible says, "Therefore He is also able to save to the uttermost those who come to God through Him" (Hebrews 7:25). Not only did God spare Rahab and her family from complete destruction, but He also saved her to the uttermost!

Some time later, God made a way for Rahab to marry into one of the most prominent families in Israel (when she married a man named Salmon). Rahab and Salmon gave birth to a son named Boaz, who later married Ruth; Boaz and Ruth (who settled in Bethlehem) became the great-grandparents of King David. Eventually, Jesus Christ, the promised Messiah and the Lamb of God, was born into the world . . . as one of Rahab's descendants!

Who would have known that Rahab—a harlot of Jericho and the woman who let down that scarlet cord—would someday be in the ancestral line of the very One in whose blood she symbolically trusted?

In a similar way, before the Israelites departed from their bondage in Egypt (40 years before the story of Rahab), the

Lord required them to hold a special Passover meal of roasted lamb and bitter herbs. The blood of the lamb was to be applied on the doorposts of each Hebrew home. All (including Jews and Gentiles) who gathered into the Hebrew homes where "the blood was applied" were spared when the death angel passed through that night.

As Christian believers today—over 3,500 years since that first Passover night and the story of Rahab, and nearly 2,000 years since Christ's final sacrifice—we also put our complete faith in God's "scarlet cord." We trust in the blood of the perfect Lamb of God, Jesus Christ; and by the power His blood, we are saved.

A hymn, written in 1899 by Lewis E. Jones says,

> "There is power, power, wonder-working power,
>   in the blood of the Lamb.
> There is power, power, wonder-working power,
>   in the precious blood of the Lamb."

Extending God's "Scarlet Cord"

Some people today don't want to talk about the blood as it sounds exclusive and makes people uncomfortable. But like Rahab, we fear the LORD and we are aware of His future judgment. We realize our personal sinfulness and the need for God's salvation, and we have put our trust in Him. Realizing this world's sinful condition, we also are telling others about God's only way of escape.

This is the essence of "missions." And for us and for our family, or "for me and my house" (see Joshua 24:15), this is what we do.

By God's grace, we are proclaiming God's only way of salvation, through the blood of His Only Son.

For us, in practical terms, it's preaching the Gospel, winning souls for Jesus, loving orphan children and widows, equipping national ministers, serving churches, and motivating families for God's Great Commission. From our perspective, "missions" is worlds away from any depressing or condemning mandate:

- **Missions is . . .** standing on a rugged platform and experiencing the incredible emotion of an entire city surrendering to Jesus Christ—with thousands of brand-new East African believers waving branches, shouting, and dancing with total abandon!

- **Missions is . . .** an elderly Russian woman bundled in a drab scarf—waiting outside for hours on a frozen windy day in St. Petersburg—then hugging and kissing us, over and over, with tears streaming down her face, as she is receiving her very first Bible.

- **Missions is . . .** tropical snorkeling, wildlife safaris, hot-air balloon rides, and exciting ministry travel to every continent on earth, including Antarctica!

- **Missions is . . .** spending time with Jesus, listening for His voice, and feeling His compassion for the lost.

- **Missions is . . .** God's great adventure—with challenges to conquer, blessings to bestow, and souls to be saved.

We invite you to join with God in His adventure! With faith like Rahab, just open up the window of your heart to His purposes for your life and for the lost. Release the "scarlet cord" of salvation through Christ's blood and may His glory extend to the nations!

**The bedrock foundation
for our call to
world missions
is the blood
of Jesus Christ.**

—Jon Dunagan

2

God's Only Way

Nothing But the Blood of Jesus

The bedrock foundation for our call to world missions is the blood of Jesus Christ. It is Christ's blood that sets Christianity apart from every other religion. In the world's eyes, Christ's blood is despised and rejected; yet according to God's Word, it is precious and powerful.

> "For the message of the cross is foolishness
> to those who are perishing, but to us
> who are being saved it is the power of God."
>
> —I Corinthians 1:18

Non-Offensive Evangelism?
(From Jon's perspective)

Years ago, I had an acquaintance with a pastor who was trying to add people to his church by making his services "user-friendly." One time, when I was visiting his congregation, I listened as this pastor encouraged his members to invite others to church in non-offensive ways.

Spontaneously, the pastor called for me to come up to the front (as a visiting evangelist) and to demonstrate

13

to the congregation how to lead someone to Jesus without using offensive words such as "the blood" or "the cross."

So I walked up to the front and just stood there . . . without saying a word.

After several minutes of awkward silence, the pastor seemed nervous and embarrassed.

Finally, I answered loud and clear, "Pastor, it is impossible to lead someone to salvation without talking about the blood and the cross!"

A few people in the congregation clapped, as I sat back down (but needless to say, I was never invited to preach at that church again).

Old hymn books are filled with choruses about Christ's precious blood and His sacrifice on the cross; yet many contemporary churches avoid this theme.

In "broad-minded" Christian churches, preaching about Christ's blood is considered controversial and unnecessary. A sermon about "the blood" sounds violent and grotesque. Serious discussions about sin, or God's salvation through Jesus Christ alone, are deemed insulting, or offensive. Some Christian churches even avoid any display of the cross. In many public settings, ministers or leaders are criticized, or harassed, for praying in the name of Jesus Christ.

Yet Christ's sacrifice, His cross, and His name are irreplaceable. His blood is our only hope.

Do all religions worship the same "God"?

Many people believe that all religions are basically the same—from Hinduism, Buddhism, or Islam, to primitive tribal Animism, or traditional Christianity—each merely an attempt for mankind (or womankind) to somehow connect with a "higher power" or "god."

The underlying belief is that all worldviews and religions are equally valid and that there are many ways to heaven. However, if there are *"100 Ways to Heaven,"* did Jesus spill His blood and suffer the most brutal death to make *"101 Ways to Heaven"*? Of course not!

The scriptures declare:

> "Nor is there salvation in any other,
> for there is no other name under heaven given
> among men by which we must be saved."

> —Acts 4:12

Sincere . . . or sincerely wrong?

Some think it doesn't matter *what* a person believes, as long as he or she is sincere. Their attitude says, "A little religion (of one kind or another) is probably a healthy addition to a well-rounded life, as long as a person doesn't get too confrontational, exclusive, or dogmatic."

Yet it was Jesus who exclusively said:

> "I am the way, the truth, and the life,
> no man comes to the Father but by me."

> -John 14:6

It is not enough to be sincere. The fact that many people *sincerely* believe something does not make that belief true, or that belief-system good.

A whole group can be deceived, and *sincerely wrong*.

Consider cult members forcing their kids to drink poisoned koolaid, suicide bombers killing innocent civilians, or concentration camp atrocities. Strong religious and political beliefs have motivated events like these; yet most moral people would consider these actions to be very wrong.

It *does* matter what we believe; and we need to believe the truth.

True Christianity is not like any other religion; in fact, it is totally different. It is not based on self-works or self-efforts, but it is a personal relationship with God, initiated by God Himself and completely paid for through the sacrificial blood of His Only Son.

In the end, won't God save everyone?

Even among some prominent Christian ministers, there is a trend toward various forms of Universalism and a hopeful ecumenical belief that in the end, everyone will ultimately be saved and everyone will go to heaven. Denying the doctrine of hell, these leaders believe that a truly loving and all-powerful God will eventually save everyone.

Yet God is the One who defines what is right. God defines love, holiness, and justice; and He alone makes the rules. God is the Designer of the universe, the Creator of mankind, and the Lamb slain from the world's foundation. God is God, and His ways are far above ours.

Is there such a thing as "Absolute Truth"?

A young Christian woman was in her first semester at college. In one class, the professor began questioning the reality of absolute truth. A debate started with most students siding with the idea that all truth is relative. After listening to several humanistic arguments, this quiet-mannered girl bravely decided to speak:

"In this room, there are thirty-five desks. You can count them yourself and see this is the truth. It doesn't matter if you believe it, or if you think that the number is relative, or if you try to reason it away; because no matter what you think, there will still be thirty-five desks!"

"In the same way, there ARE absolutes in this world, and believe-it-or-not, God's Word, as found in the Bible, is the ultimate foundation for truth."

As Christians, it is vital to know what we believe and why we believe it. Jesus is *the* way, *the* truth, and *the* life.

But, how do we know we're right?

Have you ever wondered how we, as Christians, can *know* that we are right, when billions of people strongly believe that *their* religion is right . . . and *ours* is wrong?

As we have traveled, we have met many Christians who turned to Jesus Christ from other worldviews. As we have talked with these believers, face-to-face, they have described to us how spiritually empty they felt before coming to the Lord and how desperately they were seeking for the truth.

Although some of these Christians are now facing hardships and persecution, they describe a freedom from previous fears and an inward peace and joy—knowing that their sins are forgiven by God. Listening to their testimonies has been challenging and motivating.

3 "Pillars" of our Faith

By faith, we believe in God's salvation through the blood of Jesus Christ. We cannot "scientifically prove" our salvation, nor can we literally go to heaven or hell to hear testimonies of personal salvation or damnation. But three "pillars" of our faith can give us an "assurance" of our salvation and of the truthfulness of the Gospel:

- **PILLAR #1**—We are sure of our salvation because of God's promises in the Bible. His Word is true and holy and endures forever.

- **PILLAR #2**—We can witness the godly transformation that takes place in our life and in others, after surrendering to Christ.

- **PILLAR #3**—There is an inward witness of the Holy Spirit who confirms with our spirit that we are children of God.

"The Spirit Himself bears witness with our spirit that we are children of God."

—Romans 8:16

Without God's mercy—through His blood—there's nothing left but God's judgment.

"For the life of the flesh is in the blood,
and I have given it for you upon the altar to
make atonement for your souls . . . "

—Leviticus 17:11

" . . . and without shedding of blood
there is no remission."

—Hebrews 9:22

Through Moses, God gave us the law to show the reality of sin, the final penalty for sin (death), and the sacrificial payment for sin (because we could never fulfill God's righteous requirements). In the law, God allowed the blood of innocent animals to be shed daily and on special occasions to "cover over" sin for a period of time—until the Messiah would pay the penalty for sin in full.

Throughout the Old Covenant, there were hundreds of thousands of animals offered to God as sacrifices. In one offering alone, King Solomon offered over 142,000 cattle and sheep. Imagine how much blood was shed in just that one event, not to mention all the countless other sacrifices that were offered throughout all of history. But animal sacrifices only covered the people's sins for a short time. In a sense, they only "appeased" God's wrath.

Each year, the high priest sprinkled animal blood on a place in the tabernacle (and later in the temple) called the "mercy seat"—which was on the golden lid of the Ark of the Covenant.

Inside of the Ark of the Covenant, under this mercy seat, was a copy of the law of Moses. At one point (after the ark had been returned to Israel by the Philistines in I Samuel 6:19) some of the Israelites wanted to look into the ark, but they removed the mercy seat. As a result, over 50,000 people were killed by God's power.

Do you see the picture?

If a person tried to remove God's mercy, there was nothing remaining but God's law and wrath. It was only because of the blood, sprinkled on the mercy seat by the high priest, that shielded the people from God's judgment.

God's Final Sacrifice

After Jesus died on the cross, the Bible says that Jesus took His own blood and sprinkled it on the mercy seat of heaven. He did not have to repeat this daily, weekly, or yearly, as required in the Old Testament sacrifices.

Once, and one time only, Jesus offered His blood.

Jesus' blood is more powerful than all the sacrificial blood combined throughout history. Hebrews chapter 9 declares that Christ came as our High Priest, with a greater and more perfect sacrifice, not with the blood of bulls and goats and calves, but with His own precious blood. Jesus' offering on the cross was once and for all.

As we see in Hebrews chapter 10, the blood of Jesus Christ was the final sacrifice for sins:

"By that will we have been sanctified through the offering of the body of Jesus Christ once for all."

—Hebrews 10:10

"But this Man, after He had offered one sacrifice for sins
forever, sat down at the right hand of God."

"For by one offering He has perfected forever
those who are being sanctified."

—Hebrews 10:12, 14

Before the cross, the children of Israel celebrated the
Passover every year to remember how the death angel "passed-
over" every believing home that was covered on the doorposts
by the blood of the Passover lamb.

After the cross, we as Christians celebrate Christ's final
sacrifice by taking Communion, as we remember how Jesus
Christ fully paid the final penalty price for our sins. All
previous sacrifices, including the Passover sacrifice each
year, pointed *forward* to the cross. Today, we look *back* to the
cross of Calvary and thank God that no further sacrifice is
necessary.

Why is the Blood of Jesus so Powerful?

Jesus Christ's blood was not the same as the blood of
animals, which had to be offered up continually—over-and-
over—as periodic coverings for sin.

It is by faith we believe and understand that Jesus' blood
was pure enough, life-giving enough, and strong enough.
He only had to offer it up one time.

1. Jesus' blood is powerful because He is the Creator.

As an individual, your life is in your blood; and your
blood is the life of one person only—you!

Jesus's blood is powerful, because He is the Creator!

Yet the blood of Jesus is different. Jesus Christ created all things (John 1:3) and as Creator, His blood is more valuable than all of His creation combined. Through Him, all things were made and in Him all things consist. Jesus Christ, our Creator and the Son of God, became a man (John 1:14). As the Creator, His life-blood has the creative ability to redeem all who believe upon Him.

"All things were made through Him, and without Him nothing was made that was made."

—John 1:3

"And the Word became flesh, and dwelt among us . . ."

—John 1:14

"And He Himself is the propitiation for our sins, and not for ours only but also for the whole world."

—I John 2:2

"In whom we have redemption through His blood, the forgiveness of sins. He is the image of the invisible God . . . for by Him all things were created . . . and in Him all things consist."

—Colossians 1:14-17

2. Jesus' blood is powerful because it was appointed by God to be the payment for our world's sins.

Even before the earth's creation, God knew that man would sin and would someday need a Savior. In that sense, Jesus Christ was the

"Lamb slain from the foundation of the world."

—Revelation 13:8

Both before and during the Old Testament time of the law, God accepted animal sacrifices as a temporary covering for sin until His Messiah would come. The animal sacrifices pointed the way to Jesus Christ and His ultimate final sacrifice for our sins—God Himself taking on human flesh and dying as our substitute.

"Behold! 'The Lamb of God
who takes away the sins of the world!'"

—John 1:29

Old Testament saints died in faith, believing in a future Savior and Messiah, and it was "accredited" to them (as future credit to their account) as righteousness.

They believed in the Savior *who was to come.* In the New Covenant, we believe in the Savior *who has come* and has paid the penalty for our sin in full. At the moment of our salvation, we are not just "accounted righteous." We are "made righteous" through Jesus Christ (see Romans 5:19).

Jesus' blood was appointed by God to be the payment for our world's sins.

3. The blood of Jesus Christ was sinless and His blood was the perfect sacrifice.

Jesus was tempted by Satan and accused of many things by evil men. But in John 8:46, Jesus states, "Which of you convicts me of sin?"

Paul declares in II Corinthians 5:21, that Jesus Christ " . . . knew no sin . . . "and I Peter 2:22 confirms this of Christ, "Who committed no sin . . ."

The blood of Jesus Christ was sinless. His blood was the perfect sacrifice.

Because mankind had sinned, a perfect man's blood had to pay the penalty price for sin. Yet because of sin, not one person was perfect. Every person on earth had sinned and all people had inherited a "sin-nature" from Adam.

The blood of animals could never forgive sin, but it could only "cover over" sin for a short period of time. However, because Jesus Christ came as the Son of God—fully God and fully man—His blood was perfect. Because He was born of a virgin, His only Father was God. Jesus Christ did not inherit the "sin-nature" that had been passed down, from Adam, to all of humanity and He lived a completely perfect life. Christ's blood was unique; it was (and is) sinless.

"knowing that you were not redeemed with corruptible things, like silver or gold, from your aimless conduct received by tradition from your fathers, but with the precious blood of Christ, as of a lamb without blemish and without spot."

—I Peter 1:18-19

4. Jesus' blood is powerful because it was applied on the mercy seat of heaven.

The Old Testament temple and Ark of the Covenant were only the copy and "shadow" of the original objects in heaven [the heavenly temple and the heavenly Ark of the Covenant] (Hebrews 8:5). In this verse, God also explains to Moses the importance of following His divine instructions in making these special objects.

"For He said, 'See that you make all things according to the pattern shown you on the mountain.'"

In the Old Testament, the high priest would sprinkle the sacrificial blood of animals upon the mercy seat. Inside of the ark was a copy of God's law which had been given to Moses (along with a portion of manna and Aaron's rod which had budded). Through God's law we understand how wicked and unrighteous we truly are and through the example of the sacrificial animals offered on the mercy seat of the Ark of the Covenant, we see a glimpse of God's required payment for sin.

The only way for people to be accepted before God was for innocent blood to be shed as a covering (or as an "atonement") for sin. In the Old Testament, God allowed animal blood to "cover" sins, but only for short periods of time. This sacrificial animal blood had to be sprinkled often, over-and-over, to satisfy God's wrath. Yet when Jesus died, He took His own pure blood to sprinkle in the true temple and on the true mercy seat and on the true Ark of the Covenant in heaven—to pay the final penalty for our sin.

Jesus' blood is powerful, because it was applied on the mercy seat of heaven.

"Not with the blood of goats and calves, but with His own blood He entered the Most Holy Place once for all, having obtained eternal redemption."

—Hebrews 9:12

Jesus' blood not only "covered over" the judgment of the law, but He wiped away the sin penalty that we deserved. Jesus Christ disarmed Satan from his ability to condemn us for our sins (Romans 8:1) and He has made us "new creatures" in Him (II Corinthians 5:17).

And as a final testimony of this Old-Covenant to New-Covenant transition, the thick veil in the temple in Jerusalem—which separated the Holy of Holies and the Ark of the Covenant from the rest of the temple (and which separated God's presence from the rest of the world)-was torn in two, from top to bottom.

It was finished.

God's final sacrifice had been made and the way to His salvation was open for all of mankind.

Through the ultimate sacrifice of His own perfect blood offered on the mercy seat of heaven, Jesus Christ made the way for us to draw near to God—forever.

What can wash away our sins?
Nothing but the blood of Jesus!
What can make me whole again?
Nothing but blood of Jesus!

It's why our Lord suffered and died on the cross; and it's why He now commands us to take up our cross and to follow Him—so others can know His love, and be saved.

A few notes about heaven and hell:

From *Radical*, by David Platt:

> If people will go to heaven simply based on
> their native religious preferences, then there is no
> urgency for any of us to go to them. But if they will
> not go to heaven because they have never heard of
> Christ, then there is indescribable urgency for all of
> us to go to them. (p. 143)
>
> —From Chapter 7, "There Is No Plan B"

From *Erasing Hell*, by Francis Chan & Preston Sprinkle:

> A sense of urgency over the reality of hell
> should recharge our passion for the gospel as
> it did for Paul, who, "knowing the fear of the Lord,"
> persuaded people to believe (2 Corinthians 5:11).
> We should not just try to cope with hell, but be
> compelled—as with all doctrine—to live differently
> in light of it." (p. 147)

> While hell can be a paralyzing doctrine, it can
> also be an energizing one, for it magnifies the beauty
> of the cross . . .

> Hell is the backdrop that reveals the
> profound and unbelievable grace of the cross. It
> brings to light the enormity of our sin and therefore
> portrays the undeserved favor of God in full color.
> Christ freely chose to bear the wrath that I deserve
> so that I can experience life in the presence of God.
> (p. 148)

**I have seen the Vision
And for self I cannot live.
Life is less than worthless,
Till my all I give.**

—Oswald J. Smith,
Missionary Evangelist

3

God's Vision

Big Questions about World Missions

For many Christians, "missions" is, at best, a necessary responsibility. For hundreds of years the church has always "supported the missionaries," and so tradition continues— yet often without God's heart and passion or even a compelling purpose to win the lost to faith in Jesus Christ.

No wonder then, when many of us think of a missionary, strange images come to mind!

You may picture some young adventurer—clad in khaki safari clothes—trudging through the jungles with a machete. Perhaps you imagine him (or her) meeting a group of dark-skinned natives, dancing around mud huts and a raging fire, all moving to the beat of a pounding tribal drum.

Or maybe your only view of a missionary is of some strange older couple, in outdated clothing, presenting never-ending blurry slides or a shaky home video for some "special" Sunday evening service. Completing this picture are uninspiring stories of terrible food and awful living conditions, ending with a dreaded drawn-out plea for money. Perhaps it's time, for the sake of the lost, to change our pictures of missions today.

Big Question #1:
Is there still a need for world missions?

The word mission brings to mind definitions such as goal, vision, and purpose. As Christians, what is God's purpose for our lives? What are His goals and vision?

- **Our primary calling . . .** is to know and love the Lord. But if that were all, God could have taken us to heaven the moment we received Jesus Christ.

- **Our primary mission . . .** is to glorify God in and through our lives and to help make God's way of salvation known throughout the earth.

With our primary mission clearly in view, we can see the need to help proclaim the Gospel of Jesus Christ and obey God's words to "Go into all the world."

We need to ask ourselves if we really believe the Bible is the true and inspired Word of God.

Do we honestly believe people must be saved, or "born again," as Jesus said in John 3:3, and can we comprehend the eternal reality of heaven and hell? If we do, these beliefs should radically impact our lives.

Think for a moment about how different your life would be if you were born in a land isolated from the Gospel and filled with extreme poverty and disease.

What would it be like if you were born in an area where praying to an idol or giving homage to an ancestor was your only hope? What if constant fear of evil spirits consumed your life? Wouldn't you want someone to share God's life-giving message with you?

We have received God's light, but it is not just for us. We are called to shine God's light in the darkness.

For those of us who live in developed countries, we need to realize how much God has blessed us:

- **We are blessed!** Every day we enjoy clean, hot running water—without a thought.

- **We are blessed!** Our typical meals include many ingredients from around the world: fruit from California and the Polynesian islands, olive oil from Italy and the Middle East, and coffee from Columbia (just try looking at your food labels for a few days). We eat better than the ancient kings!

- **We are blessed!** Most of us, with a few quick calls to a travel agency and a credit company could likely travel next month to any destination in the world, if we really wanted to (not that we're advocating debt, but if reaching people is a top priority, budgets can be made to accommodate).

God has given us the greatest "Good News" of all time and a job description to "Get this news out!" He has given us an abundance of resources to accomplish the task and a challenge that,

We are blessed to be a blessing!

> "To whom much is given, from him much will be required."
>
> —Luke 12:48

Big Question #2:
Why go overseas when we have so many needs in our own country?

Missionary evangelist Oswald J. Smith answered this question with another: "Why should anyone hear the Gospel twice before everyone has heard it once?"

We do have needs, but ours pale in comparison, according to the *World Christian Encyclopedia:*

- **The missions need:** In North America there are more than one million full-time Christian workers (one full-time Christian leader for every 230 people), while in many places there is only one missionary for every 500,000 people!

- **The missions need:** Since the invention of the printing press in 1450, 85 percent of all Bibles ever printed have been printed in English—yet only 9 percent of the world speaks English as a primary language! About 80 percent of the world's people have never owned a Bible, yet in the United States, there is an average of four Bibles in each household!

- **The missions need:** Many of us hear the Gospel repeatedly, while approximately 1.6 billion people are still waiting for their first opportunity to hear.

- **The missions need:** Even among Christian missionaries, only 15 percent of mission finances are used for Gospel work among "unreached" people. *Revolution in World Missions* states that nearly 80 percent of missionaries are involved primarily in social work, not in proclaiming the Gospel, winning souls, or establishing churches. For heaven's sake-literally-what did Jesus call us to do?

Big Question #3:
Aren't all cultures equally valid? Why should we try to "change" other people's cultures?

The core issue of this question stems from a false application of "multiculturalism"—one that is politically correct, educationally encouraged, and sounds nice. But leaving people trapped in sin and isolated from God's hope of salvation isn't the "considerate" option.

As Christians, we bring the cross-cultural, life-changing message of Jesus Christ and His forgiveness for sin. Our purpose is not to propagate our personal cultural standards, but to present the Gospel in a redeeming yet culturally sensitive way to all people. Eliminating the uniqueness of international culture is not the purpose of Christian missionary work; at times, however, sinful elements of a particular culture may need to change.

Years ago, we had an interview with an outstanding Christian teenager who attended a public high school. This young man led a lunchtime Bible Club and worship time that grew to reach 250 of his fellow classmates. He was writing a school research paper on Christian missionary work; and specifically, he was trying to support his thesis that "modern missionaries do not attempt to 'change' foreign cultures."

We understood this young man's heart.

This teenager was trying to explain how today's Christian missionaries are different—more culturally appreciative and sensitive—than some of the old-time colonial missionaries (who attempted to expand all aspects of Western civilization throughout the world).

But we still disagreed with his conclusion.

We asked this young man a pointed question. "But don't you try to 'change the culture' of the people you are trying to reach?

Just look at the typical 'culture' of the teens in your high school before they come to Jesus Christ! Look at the way they dress! Listen to their music, their foul language, and the way they address their teachers! What about the videos they watch and the movies they sneak into? What about typical teenagers involved in sexual impurity or the girls who have had abortions? Aren't all of these a part of teen 'culture'?"

We went on to explain to him, "Culture is life!"

When you share Jesus Christ in your high school, of course you don't want your friends to stop being teenagers—that's who they are! But you do want Jesus Christ to totally transform the way they live and the way they make their decisions!"

Around the world, societies that have developed isolated from God's laws and the Gospel are filled with sinful cultural elements:

- tribal hatred, ancestral worship, and idolatry

- immoral sex, adultery, and prostitution

- drug addiction, drunkenness, and witchcraft

- abuse and neglect of women and children

As Christians, our job is to bring the light of Jesus to every precious culture. Through His Word and His Holy Spirit, God will show people the changes they need to make to redeem their cultures back to Him.

Big Question #4:
Why go to remote foreign tribes? Wouldn't they be "better off" just left as they are?

Our answer to that question is a loud "No! No! No!" The unreached are never better off without Jesus Christ! Often we are blinded to this fact by a movie-world version of a "tropical native paradise." Some influential films and books portray remote tribes living in "peaceful bliss and harmony" until some "big, bad missionary" comes on the scene.

But this paradise is only an illusion! By God's grace, our family has personally ministered in over 100 nations on all seven continents--from remote villages to crowded inner cities. Throughout these missionary travels, we have never seen this "tropical native paradise."

At times, the land and beaches are beautiful and people may be warm and friendly; yet lives without God are always filled with misery.

- **In the Philippines . . .** we remember walking through a squatters village and seeing streams of human waste flowing openly down a path. We were horrified to watch a group of children toss a bucket of garbage into an already dirty river, jump into the middle of it, and start throwing the garbage on each other. These poor children were just playing, oblivious to the filth and potential for disease. Although yes, it was tropical, it was so far from God's garden of Eden!

- **In Central America . . .** we saw people crawl on bloody bare knees in penance for their sins. We sadly watched as crowds of poor, devoted people surrendered large sums of money just to carry a religious icon. These people were desperate for God's forgiveness, but as we looked into their faces, we saw no joy.

- **In Uganda . . .** we once ministered to a people group who actually worshipped a large tree. This particular tribe of people were aware of their sins and even the need for the shedding of innocent blood; yet their religion gave them no hope. They blindly offered animal sacrifices to this tree, and as we were told, at times, even human sacrifices of their young children.

- **In Tanzania . . .** one morning, we were in a remote city when we heard some terrifying news. Radical Muslims had bombed the city grounds where our mission team was scheduled to sing, preach, and show the JESUS film. In the process, these terrorists had destroyed a primary school-instantly killing eight children and seriously wounding eighty others (many who eventually died)—all to protest the message of Christianity.

- **Across the globe and through history . . .** twisted religious beliefs (such as the Hindu reverence of the cow and the rat) have caused self-inflicted food shortages and starvation. Many people groups are bound by fear, controlled by witchcraft, or filled with tribal hatred.

All over the world, individuals without Christ are separated from God by sin and are destined to spend eternity even further separated from Him—unless they hear and respond to God's Good News! But our Lord Jesus came to destroy this barrier of sin. On the cross, He surrendered His perfect life and sacrificed His sinless blood so that all people could have access to God's eternal life in heaven.

The entire message of the Bible can be summarized in words, which we all likely know by heart:

"For God so loved the world that He gave His only begotten Son, that whoever believes in Him should not perish but have everlasting life."

—John 3:16

This is the Gospel message, and our mission is to share it! We must share the blessings God has given to us; we must share our time, our talents, and our finances; and most of all, we must share our faith!

Big Question #4:
Are the lost really lost?

In the movie, *Anne of Avonlea,* our family enjoys a scene where two elderly friends, Marilla Cuthbert and Rachel Lynde, are knitting together on the front porch of Anne's house, Green Gables.

As Mrs. Lynde refers to some "heathenness" murder trials from a Boston newspaper, she declares, "Can you imagine that new minister, going on about how he doesn't believe that all the heathen will be eternally lost? The idea! If they won't be, all the money we've been sending to the foreign missions will be completely wasted, that's what!"

It's a simple excerpt, but a big issue.

As Christians, what we believe about the spiritual and eternal condition of the "lost" and the "heathen" greatly affects our attitude toward world missions.

The word "heathen" is now considered an outdated term, with negative and politically incorrect connotations; yet this word's meaning delves deep into our core theology of world missions. The term refers not only to people who are unsaved but specifically to "unreached people who have never heard the Gospel."

Is our true motivation for world missions to share the Good News of Jesus Christ with those who have yet to hear it, or do we merely want poor people to live a better life? What makes God's calling to reach the world any different than a government assistance program or a secular benevolence outreach?

Unreached people are not innocent; they have, (like us) sinned against God.

The core distinction is our belief about the lost and especially our convictions about these people who have never heard the Gospel.

Are these lost people *really* lost, or does God have an "alternative way" for them to be saved? The question makes us very uneasy and very uncomfortable. We wonder, "How could a good God send people to hell just because they've never heard the Gospel?"

It seems so unfair.

But to answer this question, we need to look beyond what we think and what we feel about fairness to what we can know from the Bible, God's Word.

First of all, people are not separated from God because they have never heard the Gospel; people are separated from God because of sin. This sin includes both the sins we ourselves commit and the "sin nature" that has been passed down to all humanity ever since Adam and Eve's fall in the garden of Eden.

When Jesus died on the cross, He paid the penalty price for both our sins (our transgressions) and our human sin nature and evil tendencies (our iniquities).

"He was wounded for our transgressions,
He was bruised for our iniquities."

-- Isaiah 53:5

The lost in foreign countries are not innocent. They have sinned and will be judged before our absolutely perfect holy God. We can trust God to judge righteously, and we can trust what He has shown us in His Word.

The Bible tells us, "For all have sinned..." (Romans 3:23) and deep down, everyone knows it.

Even without any knowledge of God's laws and the Gospel message, a person inwardly knows that he or she has done wrong things. Every person has violated the inborn, God-placed convictions of his or her own conscience (although some have become so calloused that they no longer feel remorse or guilt). This inborn realization of sin is one reason why much of humanity is so religious. Around the world, people are desperately trying to do something about their sin (even if they are merely trying to ignore God's existence!).

So are those without the Good News *really* lost, or can a person's "ignorance" of the Gospel exempt him or her from the consequences of sin? Consider the second alternative: If total ignorance (of the message of God's salvation through Jesus Christ) was an alternative way to heaven, why wouldn't it be best to keep everyone ignorant? With this reasoning, if everyone was ignorant, then everyone could be spared! Why not take it a step further and destroy all Bibles and eliminate evangelism? Then the entire world could be "saved" through this "guaranteed-ignorance exemption."

But obviously, this is not God's way.

If before the Gospel came everyone was "ignorant" (but on their way to heaven), and after the Gospel came everyone would have "knowledge" of God's salvation (but then could be condemned to hell), then wouldn't the Good News message actually be Very Bad News to a previously unreached people group?

But Jesus Christ knew—more than any of us could ever know—that salvation through His perfect blood was (and is) mankind's only hope. On the night before He was crucified, in Gethsemane, Jesus desperately cried to His Father, "If it is possible, let this cup pass from Me; nevertheless, not as I will, but as You will."

But it was not possible.

If there was any other way for mankind to besaved, then why did God allow Jesus to go to the cross? It is because there was (and is) no other way.

Without God's salvation—on His terms, and only through the saving blood of His Son—the "lost" are desperately and completely lost.

Only the blood of Jesus Christ can take away (or bring remission for) sin and pay the mercy-price before God (or make atonement) for the consequences of sin.

This fact led Jesus to the cross. This fact motivated early missionaries to leave their homelands with no hope of return. This fact was a passionate force behind the sacrificial giving of previous generations. And today, this fact motivates many Christians for world missions.

The fact is, without Jesus, the lost are lost.

The "heathen" must hear. This fact should compel us to our knees, and draw us to the nations.

Is it fair? No.

Is it fair that Jesus had to die in our place? No.

Is it fair that we sit in our churches week after week, and year after year . . . when multitudes have never once heard that Jesus even came?

Is it fair that we sit on our padded pews, critiquing our pastor's polished sermons, while 1.6 billion people have never heard even one rugged Gospel message?

No. It is not fair.

But God is totally good and holy and just. He has never been "obligated" to save the heathen and He was not "obligated" to save us!

The "heathen" must hear. This fact should compel us to our knees and draw us to the nations.

It is only because of God's great grace that He offers us His salvation, and because of God's great love that He passionately urges and compels us to proclaim His salvation—God's great news!

**The Great Commission
is not an option to consider;
it is a command
to be obeyed.**

—Hudson Taylor

4

God's Great Commission
Our Biblical Basis for World Missions

Matthew 28:19-20 and Mark 16:15 are often referred to as "The Great Commission." These final words of Jesus (before He ascended into heaven) were to "Go therefore and make disciples of all the nations" and to "Go into all the world and preach the Gospel."

These verses are often memorized and sometimes overly familiar; but our biblical basis for missions reaches far beyond these two verses! God's heart for the world—and our obligation as His followers to take the gospel to the ends of the earth—is a central theme throughout the entire Word of God.

Like Rahab's scarlet cord, we see God's mercy and grace extended for all who are covered by the blood of the Lamb—from Genesis to Revelation.

We see our first glimpse of this "scarlet cord" when the Lord clothed Adam and Eve with the skins of an innocent animal after sin enters the world.

We see it during the Passover deliverance, as God saved the Israelites by instructing them to put the blood of a lamb over their doorways and specified a way for the "strangers" (or the Gentiles) living among them to celebrate the Passover (see Exodus 12:48).

We see it in the book of Daniel as God revealed Himself to the mighty kings of Babylon and Persia; and see it interwoven through the prophecies of Isaiah and Jeremiah. This "scarlet cord" is found in God's unrelenting call to Jonah and the people of the wicked city of Nineveh, and throughout many of David's psalms.

Jesus' Heart for All Nations

It's true that a person's last words are important, but God's heart and focus did not suddenly change as Jesus Christ ascended into heaven. As He rose into the clouds, it wasn't as if Jesus dropped some last-minute change of plans on his followers: "Oh, by the way, there's just one major thing I forgot to tell you . . . "

When Jesus came to earth, His birth was announced to Jews (the shepherds) and to Gentiles (the wise men), as an angel brought "good tidings of great joy, which will be to all people" (Luke 2:10). As Jesus was dedicated in the temple, Simeon's prophetic words included, "My eyes have seen Your salvation which You have prepared before the face of all peoples, a light to bring revelation to the Gentiles" (Luke 2:30-32).

During Jesus' first recorded sermon, in the city of Nazareth, He included two Old Testament examples of God's heart for Gentiles: God's provision through Elijah for a widow of Zarephath and God's healing through Elisha for Captain Namaan of Syria. Along with these examples, Jesus read a prophecy from Isaiah and then said, "Today this Scripture is fulfilled in your hearing" (Luke 4:21). Jesus was claiming to be the Messiah—of both Jews and Gentiles—a concept totally contrary to Israel's preconceived ideas of nationalistic patriotism. For generations, the Jewish people had longed for their Promised Messiah to deliver them from other nations and to bring them glory. It's no wonder that the people of Nazareth wanted to throw Jesus over a cliff!

Throughout His earthly ministry, Jesus revealed God's heart for all people. Yes, He was sent first to the lost sheep of Israel; but He also ministered hope to a Samaritan woman, healed a Roman centurion's servant, delivered a Gadarene demoniac and fed four thousand people in a Gentile area. Even while on the cross, one of His final acts of ministry was to offer God's salvation to an undeserving thief.

Jesus taught with stories and analogies that conveyed God's love for the whole world. He called for laborers in the harvest. He commanded His disciples to launch deep and to fish for men. He challenged His followers to welcome more guests to the wedding. Jesus told of a shepherd earnestly searching for a lost sheep, a woman stopping everything to look for a lost coin, and a loving father embracing a prodigal son.

Jesus also said:

"There will be more joy in heaven over one sinner who repents than over ninety-nine just persons who need no repentance."

—Luke 15:7

If lost sinners matter that much to God, and to the angels in heaven, they should matter to us!

The Great Confusion

One day, our son was carving a wooden plaque highlighting the Great Commission from Mark 16:15. Using a friend's Bible, he wanted to check the spelling of a few words and was shocked as he searched in vain for the verses. He came to us wondering why a Bible had left out an entire page from the gospel of Mark, especially a page with such important verses about world missions.

The "Missing" Mission Verses:
(Mark 16:9-12)

"Now when He rose early on the first day of the week, He appeared first to Mary Magdalene, out of whom He had cast seven demons. She went and told those who had been with Him, as they mourned and wept. And when they heard that He was alive and had been seen by her, they did not believe.

After that, He appeared in another form to two of them as they walked and went into the country. And they went and told it to the rest, but they did not believe them either. Later He appeared to the eleven as they sat at the table; and He rebuked their unbelief and hardness of heart, because they did not believe those who had seen Him after He had risen.

And He said to them, 'Go into all the world and preach the Gospel to every creature. He who believes and is baptized will be saved; but he who does not believe will be condemned.

And these signs will follow those who believe: In My name they will cast out demons; they will speak with new tongues; they will take up serpents; and if they drink anything deadly, it will by no means hurt them; they will lay hands on the sick, and they will recover.'

So then, after the Lord had spoken to them, He was received up into heaven, and sat down at the right hand of God. And they went out and preached everywhere, the Lord working with them and confirming the word through the accompanying signs. Amen."

In many Bibles, a little fine-print "disclaimer" right below Mark chapter 16 often brings confusion regarding the validity of these important verses. Some translators attempt to discredit the Great Commission by stating, "Mark chapter 16, verses 9-20 were not included in the two most reliable ancient Greek manuscripts: the Codex Sinaiticus and Codex Vaticanus."

Those theological words sound official and beyond the expertise of an average Bible-believing Christian. For most of us, we simply need to know that God's Word is true and that the Great Commission is a real calling of God, to be followed and obeyed. So, if you read one of these "Great Commission disclaimers," please note a few additional facts these theological scholars *don't* tell you:

- These same "most reliable manuscripts" leave out many portions of the Bible (for example, the Codex Vaticanus leaves out Genesis 1-46, Psalm 105-137, Hebrews 9:14 to 13:25, 1 and 2 Timothy, Titus, Philemon, and Revelation). Why discredit the verses in Mark, without discrediting the others?

- Mark 16:9-20 appears in the vast majority of ancient Bible manuscripts (of the 618+ Greek manuscripts with the Gospels, only two do not have these verses.)

- These verses from Mark were quoted by important church fathers (such as the Ante-Nicene Fathers) whose writing predates these two manuscripts.

- The doctrine of the Great Commission is consistent with scripture. It can be also found in all of the other three Gospels and in the book of Acts (see Matthew 28:19, Luke 24:47, John 20:21 and Acts 1:8).

We once heard a powerful personal testimony from a missionary in Communist China.

In one remote village, a national minister had access to only one page from a Bible: and it was the final page of the Gospel of Mark. With these "questionable" verses as his only scripture, this Chinese minister had preached the message of God's salvation, led many people to believe in the Lord, witnessed miracles and healings, and a resulting Christian fellowship had begun, leading others to faith in Jesus Christ.

In time, these believers gathered together and grew into a church. These Great Commission scripture verses were "life" to them, and life-changing to many!

The Early Church and World Missions

Throughout the New Testament we see God's "scarlet cord" of salvation—from Philip preaching to the Samaritans and the Ethiopian in Acts 8, Peter bringing the gospel to Cornelius and his friends and family in Acts 10, in Paul's letters to churches comprised of both Jews and Gentiles, and concluding with John's end-time vision of "a great multitude which no one could number, of all nations, tribes, peoples, and tongues" worshipping together before God's throne in heaven (Revelation 7:9).

Even in the map section in the back of most of our Bibles, there are usually several pages that highlight the Apostles' early missionary journeys.

It's not hard to find a biblical basis for world missions; it's hard not to see it. The "scarlet cord" theme is like a red ribbon on a Bible—it extends from cover to cover!

The Great Commission in Every Gospel and in the Book of Acts:

- **Matthew 28:19**
  "...Go therefore and make disciples of all the nations, baptizing them in the name of the Father and of the Son and of the Holy Spirit."

- **Mark 16:15**
  He said to them, "Go into all the world and preach the Gospel to every creature."

- **Luke 24:47-48**
  "...and that repentance and remission of sins should be preached in His name to all nations, beginning at Jerusalem. And you are witnesses of these things."

- **John 20:21**
  Jesus said to them again, "Peace to you! As the Father has sent Me, I also send you."

- **Acts 1:8**
  "But you shall receive power when the Holy Spirit has come upon you; and you shall be witnesses to Me in Jerusalem, and in all Judea and Samaria, and to the end of the earth."

Not, how much of my money will I give to God, but, how much of God's money will I keep for myself?

—John Wesley

5

God's Great Provision
Trusting God and Stepping Out

In our family's living room, a small homemade treasure chest displays coins from around the world: francs from France, pulas from Botswana, euros from Europe. Most are dull and worn, while others are shiny and new. Our favorite is an intricate gold-and-silver-colored piece from Italy, but (as with most of the coins) we have no idea of its worth. Some are no longer in circulation; some countries they are from no longer exist. All are simply leftover pocket-change from years of mission trips—saved as little souvenirs and little reminders that money is only a temporary "little thing." Each metal circle is (or was) valuable only because some government somewhere decided it would have value.

But money is also a "big thing." Our money represents our life. It represents our time, our talents, our education and experiences, and our priorities. In fact, if we want to find out what is really important to us, we can simply look through our checkbook or credit card statements over the past few months. Our priorities are there—in black and white—and the numbers don't lie.

The Bible says, "Where your treasure is, there your heart will be also." The reverse is also true: "Where your heart is, that's where your treasure will go."

It's very simple. If we're kingdom-minded we'll give to spread the Gospel. And as Christians, "our" money is not really ours! We need to acknowledge that everything we have belongs to God: our life is God's, our kids are God's, our home is God's, our car is God's, our money is God's. We're simply stewards of God's "stuff."

I'm not called to be a missionary, but I'll pray and I'll give . . .

You may have heard the statement, "Some are called to go, while others are called to pray and to give." We don't disagree with this statement; but if it's true, the level of commitment should be the same for all of us.

It's not uncommon to hear of a missionary "go-er" willing to surrender everything to fulfill God's call; yet have you ever heard of a "giver" willing to do the same? Do you think God only requires sacrifice from those who go? NO! We are all equally called to help fulfill God's Great Commission. As Christians we're blessed for a bigger purpose than blessing ourselves! Like Abraham, we're blessed to establish God's covenant on the earth.

If your part in the Great Commission is to pray, don't you think you should pray at *least* as much, if not *more*, than those whose primary job is to go? Unfortunantly, however, that is not often the case. Usually those who are called to "go" feel the greatest burden in the other areas as well: financially, for the needs of the mission, and spiritually, for the needs of the lost. They know they are in a spiritual battle and they have devoted their entire lives to the call.

The point is not that the "go-er's" should decrease their giving and praying, but that the "pray-er's" and "giver's" should pray and give more!

As Christians, we are all called to a life of prayer, not only to intercede for the world's needs and for the lost, but to also enjoy our personal relationship with the Lord. Never underestimate the impact (on your life and on others) by simply taking time to "be with God." Pray regularly and specifically for people you know who are lost, and for ministry leaders, pastors, and missionaries who are on the front-lines of advancing God's kingdom.

10 reasons to PRAY daily for the lost:

- 1.   Prayer increases your love for others.
- 2.   Prayer increases your boldness to witness.
- 3.   Prayer helps people to become convicted of sin.
- 4.   Prayer causes spiritual "blinders" to come down.
- 5.   Prayer helps bring "divine contacts" to others.
- 6.   Prayer opens opportunities to share our faith.
- 7.   Prayer helps us to know God's direction.
- S.   Prayer releases people from Satan's control.
- 9.   Prayer helps us to be more sensitive to needs.
- 10.   Prayer is commanded by God.

If your part in the Great Commission is to pray or to financially support world missions, then trust God to increase your level of commitment. Begin to think (and to dream) about what your prayers and your resources could do for God. Instead of endlessly browsing through shopping malls and catalogs, be "on the lookout" for projects and people that God may want you to help.

Of course we must provide for our families, but as stewards of the Great Commission we must be willing to abandon the typical American dream, for God's dream!

If your income is limited, seek God for creative ways to save or raise money for missions. You could have a yard sale, lead a car wash, organize a fund-raiser, forgo a daily espresso, or encourage children to collect coins in a "missions jar." Challenge yourself, your church, or your family. In many developing countries, your modest savings or increased income—of even a few dollars a day (from your family's mission projects)—could fully support a national missionary or an orphan child!

But what if I am called to go? How can I know that God will provide?

Your modest savings could fully support a national missionary or an orphan child.

Perhaps you once considered the possibility of going on a mission trip—either for a short-term outreach or for long-term service—but the thought of somehow raising financial support made you break into a cold sweat and turned your stomach in knots; so, you decided to give up the idea all together.

But, was that what God wanted?

Imagine the confusion and distraction if every soldier in the military had to worry about his or her own support:

- How will I get to the frontline?
- What if I can't afford my uniform?
- Where will I sleep, and what will I eat?
- Who will provide for my family?

II Timothy 2:4 says, "No one engaged in warfare entangles himself with the affairs of this life." God's kingdom-advancing resources are far beyond what any earthly commander-in-chief could ever dream of; but God wants His heavenly soldiers to seek souls and His kingdom purposes, not money! If God calls you into His service, it may mean sacrifice; but you can trust Him to meet all of your needs. Ultimately, "Where God guides, He provides. Where He leads, He meets the need."

Experiencing God's provision is an exciting way to live, but it can be a frightening adventure when you first step out of your comfort-zone and learn to rely on Him.

The Story of the Blue Lamp

(From Ann's perspective):

Jon and I were 21-years-old and just completing our university and Bible college degrees when the Lord began training us to totally rely on Him. At the time, we were preparing to move from Oklahoma to Oregon to step out into "full-time" ministry. In prayer, we felt the Lord was calling us to focus on evangelism and world missions, and specifically, Jon felt that he was not to work any other job (for pay) outside of the ministry.

We had accumulated a modest savings and were selling our belongings; but no matter how many times we tried to calculate our budget, there was no natural way, financially speaking, it would work. Even if all of our possessions sold for "top-dollar," we wouldn't have any money to live on, beyond the first few months. We didn't have any incoming ministry support and we didn't know anyone in the city where we were headed. The more we thought about it, and tried to rearrange the numbers, the more concerned and frustrated we became.

As graduation drew near, Jon began to earnestly seek God for direction and provision. One day, after a time of prayer, he came in and said to me: "Honey, you'd better sit down..."

He then unloaded what could have been a "bomb" on a young wife: "Ann, I believe God wants us to forsake everything and to totally depend on Him—and not on ourselves. Just as the disciples left their nets to follow Jesus, I believe God wants us to give away our (only) car, all of our savings, and everything we've had for sale."

For a moment, I let the words sink in . . .

It sounded crazy, but somehow, God instantly "confirmed" his words in my heart—and I agreed.

Inside, I somehow knew it was what God wanted. Besides, if it was God, it would work; and if it wasn't, we shouldn't be in ministry! A "faith" dropped into my heart that was unexplainable. All worry and anxiety left, and Jon and I were both instantly filled with excitement.

That night, we called a few friends and told them to come over and take anything they wanted. The next day, we gave our car to a fellow Bible school student who had wanted to buy it, and in the next church offering, we gave our entire savings. We gave a beautiful hand-carved wooden baby crib to a woman I had prayed with (who, by the way, had been barren, but was now expecting!), and, most difficult of all, I presented our church worship director with a treasured silver flute which my parents had sacrificially bought for my sixteenth birthday.

Now, there was no possible way we could step out in ministry on our own. If it worked, it would be the Lord's provision . . . and we just knew it would work!

But two days before we were to move, reality "hit." We had nothing. The lease was up on our apartment. Our church had already prayed for us and "sent us out." We had no vehicle and no money.

- How would we live?
- How were we going to get across the country?
- Could we expect someone to GIVE us a car?

Jon looked at me, sleeping on the floor with our newborn baby, and suddenly felt a wave of despair, personal responsibility, and condemnation. Desperately, he cried out to the Lord in prayer,

"God, did I hear You right?"

As he prayed, he felt a reassuring peace, and a still small voice: "Yes, and as soon as you do everything I've told you to do, you'll see My provision."

All morning, Jon kept asking me if there was something we hadn't yet done, but we couldn't think of anything... Finally, we got out our "For Sale" list and went down the items one-by-one, until we came to:

"Blue Lamp - $5."

Looking across the room, we saw the little blue lamp sitting on a cardboard box in the corner. We had found it at a garage sale (originally an ugly-orange color), and had painted it country-blue. "The lamp! The lamp!" we both shouted. "We forgot to give away the lamp!"

Immediately, Jon grabbed that little blue lamp— along with a handful of pots and pans—and headed to our neighbor's apartment. Our young bachelor-friend probably didn't know what to think when Jon loaded his arms with the strange combination, saying, "Here! God wants you to have these!"

Jon hurried back to our apartment, and—with no exaggeration—about three minutes later we received a phone call from a man we barely knew:

"Is this Jon Dunagan?"

"Yes."

"Do you need a car?"

Jon attempted to conceal his growing excitement:

"Uh, why do you ask?"

Before, we had been trusting in ourselves ...but now, we were totally depending on God.

"Well, my wife and I have been feeling that God wants us to give you our car. We've never done anything like this before, so we prayed about it all last night. It wasn't until just a few minutes ago that we finally felt a peace about calling you."

That last step of obedience—giving that insignificant blue lamp—released God's provision! Before, we had been trusting in ourselves and our "stuff," but now we were totally depending on God. Within two days, we left for Oregon—arriving in town with our little car, a few dishes, some clothes, one baby, and $27!

We began preaching in parks and witnessing on the streets, and a city-center roller-skating rink allowed us to use their building—completely free of charge—for weekly church services! The local economy at the time was so slow, we even found a nice four-plex apartment with a remarkable special:

"Move-in today, and don't pay (for three months)!"

Our First Mission Trip

After a short time in Oregon, God led us to a pastor who helped arrange our first overseas mission trip: to Hong Kong, Macau, China, and the Philippines.

The Lord provided money for our family's airline tickets, but when it came time to leave, we didn't have any money for traveling expenses—not even enough money for gas to get to the airport!

Here we were, a young couple with an 18-month-old baby, and I was seven months pregnant! Our overseas contacts were complete strangers and we didn't know if we would need to pay for our own expenses once we were there.

- How could we leave with no money?
- Would we be a blessing, or a burden?
- Was it really God's will?

As we prayed together, God again gave us a peace that could only come from Him.

We were actually holding a globe as God gave us a heavy burden for the lost in these specific countries, and the Lord reassured us that He could provide for us *there* (as we pointed to Asia) just as easily as He could provide for us *here* (as we pointed to the United States). From God's perspective, there was no difference; but to us, it was an important lesson in trust.

We decided to pack our car and drive towards the airport until our near-empty gas tank ran out. Right before we left, we took one last check in our apartment and saw a recent message on our answering machine:

"Hey, Jon and Ann, if you haven't left yet, I've got 'something' for you at the church..."

That 'something' was a twenty-dollar bill. It was enough to get us to the airport!

En route to Asia, we had an opportunity to share at a church meeting in Hawaii. Unexpectedly, they took a missions offering for us, and we were on our way! On the outreach, no one knew of our financial situation. Every step along the way we had enough money to pay for every expense and need. We were able to monetarily bless our ministry contacts and we even came home with souvenirs! We saw firsthand the "ripe harvest" overseas, and our lives have never been the same!

How does a missionary build a support base?

As Betty Barnett of YWAM wrote in her excellent book, this is a process of *Friend Raising* not fund-raising. When stepping out into ministry or missionary work, one of the first steps-while praying and seeking the Lord-is to build a support base for prayer, mutual encouragement and financial partnership.

Stepping out into full-time ministry or mission work may require dying to your self-righteous pride, and reevaluating self-sufficient attitudes. Sometimes we inwardly think: there's NO way I would ever take money from people I know. If God provides "supernaturally" that's one thing, but I will never be like some beggar . . . just mooching off friends and family!

Do we consider trusting God and "living by faith" equivalent to relying on government assistance? Our thoughts degrade God's calling and the obedience of His frontline warriors!

Continuing to Trust God

For more than two decades, God has faithfully and abundantly provided for us—for literally hundreds of missionary outreaches, for every ministry need, and for continual provision for our growing family.

When we have a financial need, we simply seek God's direction. Sometimes, we state a need in our monthly missions newsletter; sometimes the Lord directs us to say something to a particular person or a ministry partner. Other times, we simply pray.

I will never be like some beggar . . . just mooching off friends and family!

But quite often, when we are facing a big need, God will challenge us to generously GIVE to someone else!

Often, we do something we call "tithing in advance"; just as people in the Bible gave of their "first-fruits" (a tithe of what they hoped their crops would produce), we sometimes give ten percent of what we *need* for a missions outreach, before any money comes in!

No matter how the details work out, God always comes through, and He cares about everything, big and little! He has provided ministry vehicles and sound systems for national evangelists, support for remote missionaries, and buildings for village churches. He also has provided for "extra" personal things, like bicycles and orthodontic braces for our own kids!

God's provision doesn't always look the same, but it's always there!

One month, we trusted God and saw His provision for $15,000 for a city-wide evangelistic outreach in the country of Zaire (now Democratic Republic of Congo); but soon afterward, we felt the Lord encouraging us to trust Him to head back to Africa on another mission—without bringing one cent (using free airline tickets)!

When another "impossible" situation comes, the Lord reminds us how we began, and reassures us that He will keep meeting our needs today . . . and tomorrow!

Missions & God's Provision:

- **Missions is** . . . seeking godly counsel from your pastor, church leaders, godly mentors, or a mission organization.

- **Missions is** . . . asking if you can share your vision at your home church or at the churches of your close friends or family and setting up a table display (or putting together a video or PowerPoint presentation) with photos of people you plan to reach or maps of projected areas.

- **Missions is** . . . creating a ministry brochure, postcard, flyer, or letter, with an introduction of you and/or your family, highlights of your ministry experiences and vision for missions (with perhaps a few recommendations, and a response card and return envelope.)

- **Missions is** . . . sharing your vision, realizing that God is your source of provision—not the people. Missions is conveying your heart for the lost and talking about your future vision (and being so thankful when a minister or a friend invites people to join with you in prayer or support).

- **Missions is** . . . reading *Friend Raising* (by Betty Barnett), *Daring to Live on the Edge* (by Loren Cunningham), and *Money, Possessions, and Eternity* (by Randy Alcorn).

- **Missions is** . . . sending your first newsletter, seeking God about who to include in your mailing (making lists of relatives, church friends, co-workers, high school and college friends, Christmas card friends, and people you meet as you share your vision)— including a simple letter, a quality ministry brochure or postcard, and a handwritten note.

- **Missions is** . . . preceding your first ministry mailing with a personal contact (realizing a friendly call or note to touch base with a longtime friend can make a big difference).

**The Great Commission
is the Great Adventure
of Christianity.**

—Ron Luce

6

God's Great Adventure

Exciting Experiences from Every Continent

"For we are His workmanship, created in Christ Jesus for good works, which God prepared beforehand that we should walk in them."

—Ephesians 2:10

The following international mission testimonies are a few of our "personal adventure stories" as our family has grabbed hold of God's passion for souls, held tightly to Jesus, and let the Holy Spirit send us anywhere!

May God be glorified; may you be encouraged to step out in faith; and may many more people have opportunity to hear the Gospel message, as you live out the specific call and adventure that God has prepared for YOU!

Missions is not just for missionaries; God's call is for all!

—Jon & Ann Dunagan

AFRICA

- **Missions is** . . .traveling by canoe to an isolated island, using a pit toilet, and sleeping under a mosquito net in a mud hut!

- **Missions is** . . . having a witchdoctor publicly curse us and tell people to "Come and watch the preachers DIE!"— and because of his threats, thousands came and heard the Gospel and all witnessed total pandemonium as the witchdoctor's nearby hut suddenly caught on fire, right during the meeting, and burnt to the ground! (A local radio station documented the event saying, "During today's Gospel crusade in Morogoro [in Tanzania] a fire came from 'nowhere' and burnt down a witchdoctor's house!") For years the witchdoctor's property remained untouched; and because of the fire, many gave their lives to Jesus!

- **Missions is** . . . caring for hundreds of East African orphans, and trusting God for ongoing support.

- **Missions is** . . . preaching the Gospel and sharing about God's forgiveness in stadiums and prisons across the nation of Rwanda only months after their brutal genocide—and seeing men from the warring Hutu and Tutsi tribes publicly washing each other's feet as a symbol of repentance and reconciliation, and witnessing thousands of Rwandans from both tribes weeping, embracing, and turning to God!

- **Missions is** . . . the excitement of being chased by a bull elephant and seeing a lion close-up on a safari!

- **Missions is** . . . meeting children clothed in torn rags, remembering our cluttered closets back home, feeling God say, "I am the One naked on these streets,"—then giving armloads of clothes and being nearly crushed by desperate parents.

ASIA

- **Missions is** . . . crossing a dangerous bridge (which was closed down one week later) to preach to an isolated hilltop village in the Philippines, and being led to a man who had been in a coma for months. Even though he was unconscious, we shared the Gospel, and "led" this man in a prayer of salvation to commit his life to Jesus Christ. With the closing "Amen," color flushed into the man's body, he grabbed Jon's hand and pulled it to his chest. Smiling a huge smile, he then died. (Many were so impacted by this man's peaceful death that nearly his entire village wanted to follow Jesus!)

- **Missions is** . . . smuggling Bibles into Communist China and having guards so distracted by our blond-haired baby that they waved us past the check-point. Yet another time, having alarms go off, being called into a back room to be yelled at by armed guards, having Bibles confiscated—and getting a tiny glimpse of God's heart for the persecuted church.

- **Missions is** . . . sitting on an airplane next to a Hindu woman, but being so tired (and knowing God would "understand") Ann pulled a blanket over her head and tried to sleep. Half-way through the flight, this Hindu woman initiated a conversation. (She had never heard of Jesus and eagerly listened to the Gospel and God's salvation plan. By the end of the flight, the woman prayed to surrender her life to Jesus. Afterwards, she kept her eyes closed for a moment, and then said, "I've never felt such peace.")

- **Missions is** . . . our son and his newlywed bride, going on a exciting adventure to S.E. India (only a few months after their wedding) to encourage remote village pastors, to baptize new believers, and to pioneer a brand-new children's orphan home!

LATIN AMERICA

- **Missions is** . . . leading teams of teenagers across the Mexican border, performing street dramas, preaching with puppets, painting churches, cleaning orphanages, and going door-to-door among cardboard-covered shacks to share the Good News!

- **Missions is** . . . eating delicious enchiladas!

- **Missions is** . . . sharing about Jesus and giving Spanish Bibles to workers on a mountain-top in Ushuaia, Argentina—the most southern inhabited land in the world!

- **Missions is** . . . being directed in prayer to go to Bolivia, arriving in the high altitude city of La Paz with no previous contacts and not knowing what to do next, sitting at the airport for three hours. Then having two large men—with no luggage and who wouldn't share their names—come ask, "Can we help you?" (then direct the way to a specific local church and missionary family who needed help).

- **Missions is** . . . being invited into a poor tin-roofed shack, being welcomed with warm smiles and a gracious offer to share this family's meager meal. . . and being challenged (and convicted) by such a generous example of hospitality.

- **Missions is** . . . browsing in an outdoor market in Guatemala and bargaining for a colorful blanket!

- **Missions is** . . . witnessing in Central America during Holy Week, admiring sidewalks covered with intricate flower mosaics on Palm Sunday; seeing thousands of people in crucifixion processions on Good Friday; and on Sunday, preaching about the Resurrection!

EUROPE

- **Missions is** . . . meeting a college student on a ferry between Calais, France and Dover, England; sharing about Jesus; discussing the differences of Mormonism and Christianity; having her wonder if we were angels, and corresponding for years!

- **Missions is** . . . interceding for revival with a Norwegian pastor, preaching in Ireland, praying through the streets of Amsterdam and Rome, and grieving over a cold continent filled with blatant pornography, prostitution, and empty cathedrals.

- **Missions is** . . . dozens of European adventures in London, Amsterdam, Spain, and Portugal (en route to missions in Africa and Asia); delightful bed and breakfasts; tea-times, whirlwind tours of Big Ben, Buckingham Palace, and the Anne Frank House; learning to use the Underground Metro, and always being "on-call" to share our faith in Jesus Christ!

- **Missions is** . . . an exciting conversation about the Lord in Paris, France—on top of the Eiffel Tower!

- **Missions is** . . . leading a young Hindu man to Jesus on the shuttle bus between the Gatwick and Heathrow airports, then several years later, on the same shuttle, discovering that this man had led his entire extended family to Christ, and they were all regularly attending a strong Christian church!

- **Missions is** . . . renting a room in an Austrian casino for a Gospel outreach, giving invitations (and having most thrown away)—then having a man come to our meeting who had nearly committed suicide that very night, but in final desperation, had cried to God, looked down, and found (crumpled in the mud) our casino-meeting invitation!

NORTH AMERICA & CARIBBEAN

- **Missions is** . . . helping a Hawaiian church on the island of Molokai-assisting a carnival outreach on the 4th of July preaching in a tent, and ending the day with an island-wide fireworks display under a clear starry sky accompanied by a church choir singing patriotic hymns—and celebrating as many responded to an altar call to receive freedom in Jesus!

- **Missions is** . . . reaching out to our community through random acts of kindness—sweeping sidewalks, leading park outreaches for children, distributing Bible tracts and church invitations, and singing about Jesus in care centers for the elderly.

- **Missions is** . . . having a faithful praying friend encourage us with two words ("No Resistance!") which she had felt for us in prayer: (Immediately after her call, on a family mission trip to Jamaica, doors opened to present Christian assemblies in public schools across the country. Not one principal turned us down, and thousands of students prayed with us to surrender their lives to Jesus.)

- **Missions is** . . . riding a scooter across the island of Bermuda, seeing pale-pink houses and white-tiled roofs—and preaching the Gospel on the streets!

- **Missions is** . . . leading a VBS-style "Missionary Adventure Preparation School" camp to teach kids about missions—with passport crafts, aiplane rooms, foreign snacks, and imaginary "travel"—and seeing campers deeply impacted by Cod's love for the lost.

- **Missions is** . . . leading a Night of Prayer for all Nations in our home and seeing our living room filled with mission-minded prayer warriors and friends from several countries.

AUSTRALIA & SOUTH PACIFIC

- **Missions is** . . . witnessing to many international Australian immigrants: taxi-drivers from Lebanon, espresso-workers from China, and waitresses from India—and being amazed at their receptivity!

- **Missions is** . . . praying for remote Aborigine tribes!

- **Missions is** . . . worshiping in the Superdome with over twenty-thousand energetic Australians from across the continent and many international guests—singing "Touching Heaven, Changing Earth" and "You are my World" and experiencing the awesome presence of God!

- **Missions is** . . . a ferry ride in the Sydney Harbor!

- **Missions is** . . . getting pictures with koalas (and while on a bus ride to the wildlife park, meeting a Muslim girl from Kuwait, sharing about the love of Jesus Christ and giving her a New Testament!)

- **Missions is** . . . biking along a sandy beach on the tropical island of Moorea (in French Polynesia), handing out DVD copies of the JESUS film, giving away free Bibles, and praying with a young family to receive Jesus Christ!

- **Missions is** . . . walking in New Zealand, meeting a Christian family and praying together for the lost.

- **Missions is** . . . driving across the lush green countryside of New Zealand, seeing a man working outside and feeling the Lord's urgent call to stop and witness . . . and finding out that the man had been earnestly searching for God . . . and then having the JOY of leading him to the Lord!

ANTARCTICA

- **Missions is** . . . having a dream about Antarctica; then (after waking up) securing passage on a polar expedition ship, feeling challenged to preach on every continent within that calendar year, interceding fervently—and then fulfilling it!

- **Missions is** . . . before the trip saying, "God told us to 'preach to every creature' and we'll even preach to the penguins!"—then on the outreach, literally distributing some of our Bibles to penguins (people from Patagonia dressed up in penguin costumes!).

- **Missions is** . . . giving away Russian Bibles and scientific-creation materials to Russian crew members and well-traveled international passengers on board the ship, and having a Scottish woman ask why our faces "glowed"!

- **Missions is** . . . preaching the Gospel during the expedition ship's talent show.

- **Missions is** . . . surviving a dangerous two-day storm while traveling through the icy waters of Drake Passage!

- **Missions is** . . . meeting an adventurous (and back-slidden) expedition leader, feeling in prayer God had once called him to preach the Gospel, seeing his shocked face as we talked with him, and hearing how long ago he had been a missionary pastor in remote regions of northern Canada.

- **Missions is** . . . "accidentally" bringing Ukrainian Bibles, so when the ship "just so happened" to stop at a remote Antarctica research station, having the opportunity to witness to Ukrainian scientists—literal residents of the "uttermost parts of the earth"!

YOU'RE NEVER TOO YOUNG!

Written by our son, Joshua (when he was a little boy):

One night when I was eight years old, I was sitting in our living room, thinking about my dad. He was away on a mission trip to Africa, and I started praying for him. As I prayed, the Lord began showing me something.

I began thinking about all the people in the world who don't know Jesus and how my dad was sharing the Gospel at that very moment. Suddenly, it "hit" me how people who don't know Jesus can't go to heaven . . . they go to hell. I kept praying, and began to realize how terrible hell really is, and how people in hell are, "STUCK THERE . . . FOREVER!"

It's hard to explain what happened, but God did something inside me. I began to cry . . . for a long time . . . and it changed the way I began to think about the lost. I realized I had never led anyone to the Lord, and I prayed specifically that God would give me a chance to share with someone that week.

Afterwards, I wrote this letter:

Dear God, I love you so much.
Please let me have a canc to cher with somyon this week. Lord, you are precic to me.

From: Joshua

(Note: A few days after writing this letter, Joshua went to a local park and shared the Gospel with a young boy named Randy, and prayed with him to receive Jesus as his Lord and Savior. Two years later, Joshua was with us in Africa boldly preaching about the fire of Elijah and the cross of Jesus Christ to an intent crowd of over 10,000 people, and leading many to the Lord!)

73

IT'S NEVER TOO LATE!

Bob and Carol were nearing retirement age, but longing for something more in their lives. For many years, he had served as a pastor at a country church, and she had taught home economics. One day, feeling somewhat discouraged and searching for the Lord's direction, this couple came to our home for dinner. Jon and I shared a few exciting mission testimonies, and then invited the two of them to go to Africa to minister at a village pastor's conference.

Despite many obstacles, Bob and Carol decided to go, and their lives have never the same!

While teaching at the African conference, they were challenged by the need for discipleship and pastoral training, and after a second short-term trip they decided to move to Africa as full-time missionaries!

A few years later, on Thanksgiving, we met for dinner again; but this time we were near their home in Uganda. As we shared strange holiday food (including zebra and ostrich), Bob and Carol began sharing a few highlights from their initial years in mission work: ten new Bible schools were training national ministers throughout East Africa, over 1,500 pastors had graduated from their year-long program, mobile health clinics were ministering to the physical needs of the people, and Carol was teaching cooking and sewing skills to enable African women to help provide for their families.

As they shared about a new vision to begin an African orphanage, we remembered back to that day only a few years earlier in our living room. This incredible young-at-heart couple had wondered if God's ministry for them was over, but it had only barely begun!

THERE'S NO EXCUSE!

Nels and Lorrie believed God was calling their family into full-time overseas missionary work, even though they had many "excuses" and challenges to overcome.

At the time, Nels and Lorrie had seven children (all homeschooled), ranging in age from younger elementary kids to a son just beginning his senior year of high school. Nels's elderly mother was living with them, and Lorrie had been having health problems (due to some recent miscarriages). On top of all that, they had no financial support.

Even so, this couple felt in their hearts that God was calling their family to move to the Philippines, and to pioneer a much-needed Bible School on a remote island.

So what did they do?

They went! -with all seven kids, their 87-year-old mother and even a paraplegic friend who decided to go with them! Together they must have been quite a site as they arrived on the island of Catanduanes: seven exhausted children, luggage everywhere, Grandma with her walker and Jeff in his wheelchair!

And God was (and is) so faithful! Everyone adjusted better than expected: the Lord met their needs; the Filipino people appreciated their family's example; the tropical sunshine helped to improve Lorrie's health.

Now (many years later), they are rejoicing as their Bible school graduates have pioneered Christian churches in unreached and remote areas of the Phillipines.

Even with every excuse to stay home, Nels and Lorrie and their family . . . went!

YOU'RE NEVER ALONE!

Doris never felt a specific "call" to world missions; she simply loved the Lord and was willing to do anything. In Bible school, she heard about a great need for missionaries in Brazil and she volunteered.

For many years, Doris ministered with her husband throughout Brazil: preaching in tents, ministering in churches, teaching children and reaching the lost.

But one horrible day, everything changed. For unspeakable reasons, her husband left.

Suddenly, Doris was alone—with no support, no family, and no way to even write home to her mission supporters back in the United States to explain what had happened.

It was at this moment, in the middle of her worst nightmare, when God gave Doris a new "dream."

It was a challenge and a renewed purpose for life . . . and it started very small:

God brought Doris a baby, a little orphan child to simply take care of—for just a few days—and Doris opened her arms.

Then child-by-child, God's challenge grew.

God brought Doris many orphans, ailing babies, and abandoned children; and even with no financial backing, Doris trusted God, and took them in.

She loved them; she held them; and she cared for the sick ones through agonizing nights. And she wept as two little ones died.

She called herself their "Momma," as she searched for Christian families to adopt them.

For many years, Doris kept a handwritten journal of all the children who came through the orphanage she founded. This journal's well-worn pages carefully list 777 precious names, the dates each child came to her, and the families who embraced them as she placed each little one in the loving arms of his or her new parents.

After over fifty years of missionary work in Brazil, Doris moved to the United States to live with one of her adopted daughters and she is now surrounded by caring grandchildren.

This precious woman, Doris, attends our home church, and our family is honored to call her our friend and one of our personal missionary heroes. Many people are grateful for her inspirational life, her ministry and love for orphans and for adoption, and her continued heart and ministry in prayer.

God didn't plan for this godly woman's marriage to end with such sadness; but He prepared a powerful redemptive plan for the whole situation.

For Doris, and all 777 children, God's plan was to never leave them alone.

**The mission of the church
is missions!**

**This generation can
only reach this generation!**

**Anywhere, provided
it be forward!**

—David Livingstone

7

100 Mission Mottos
Compelling Missionary Quotes

Get motivated for God's Great Commission with these inspiring mission mottos and missionary quotes.

Ponder these powerful and compelling words. Memorize them. Recall them in prayer. Use these concise phrases in your speaking, preaching and writing. Post them as quotes on your social media sites. Teach them to your family and children.

Most importantly, ask God to give you more of His heart for world missions and for the lost as you think about these powerful, piercing thoughts—to give, to pray, to share the Gospel, to motivate others, and to GO!!!

1. A man may die leaving upwards of a million, without taking any of it upwards.
—William Fetler

2. A nation will not be moved by timid methods.
—Luis Palau

3. Anywhere provided it be forward.
—David Livingstone

4. As long as there are millions destitute of the Word of God and knowledge of Jesus Christ, it will be impossible for me to devote time and energy to those who have both.
—J. L. Ewen

5. Can't you do just a little bit more?
—**J.G. Morrison** (pleading for missionary support during the Great Depression of the 1930s)

6. Christ alone can save the world, but Christ cannot save the world alone.
—**David Livingstone**

7. Christ not only died for all: He died for each.
—**Billy Graham**

> **Expect great things from God; attempt great things for God.**
>
> —William Carey

8. Expect great things from God; attempt great things for God.
—**William Carey**

9. Go straight for souls, and go for the worst.
—**William Booth**, The Salvation Army

10. Go, send, or disobey.
—**John Piper**

11. God had an Only Son and He made Him a missionary.
—**David Livingstone**

12. God isn't looking for people of great faith, but for individuals ready to follow Him.
—**Hudson Taylor**

13. God uses men who are weak and feeble enough to lean on him.
—**Hudson Taylor**

14. God's work done in God's way will never lack God's supply.
—**Hudson Taylor**

15. He is no fool who gives up what he cannot keep to gain that which he cannot lose.
—**Jim Elliot**

> **He is no fool who gives up what he cannot keep to gain that which he cannot lose.**
>
> —Jim Elliot

16. I am destined to proclaim the message, unmindful of personal consequences to myself.
—**Count Nicolaus Ludwig von Zinzendorf**

17. I believe that in each generation God has called enough men and women to evangelize all the yet unreached tribes of the earth. It is not God who does not call. It is man who will not respond!
—**Isobel Kuhn,**
Missionary to China and Thailand

18. If God wills the evangelization of the world, and you refuse to support missions, then you are opposed to the will of God.
—**Oswald J. Smith**

19. The Progression of a Missionary Call (Hudson Taylor):

As a child, at age five:
When I am a man, I mean to be a missionary and go to China.

As a young man:
I feel I cannot go on living unless I do something for China.

Later in life, as a veteran missionary:
If I had 1,000 lives,

I'd give them all for China.
—Hudson Taylor,
Missionary to China

20. I have but one candle of life to burn, and I would rather burn it out in a land filled with darkness than in a land flooded with light.
—John Keith Falconer

21. I have but one passion: It is He, it is He alone. The world is the field and the field is the world; and henceforth that country shall be my home where I can be most used in winning souls for Christ.
—Count Nicolaus Ludwig von Zinzendorf

22. I have seen the Vision and for self I cannot live; Life is less than worthless till my all I give.
—Oswald J. Smith

23. It is easier to be an excessive fanatic than to be consistently faithful, because God causes an amazing humbling of our religious conceit when we are faithful to Him.
—Oswald Chambers

24. I pray, and I obey.
—Yonggi Cho

25. I want to be where there are out and out pagans.
—Francis Xavier

26. I would rather die for Christ than rule the whole earth.
—Ignatius

27. If a commission by an earthly king is considered an honor, how can a commission by a Heavenly King be considered a sacrifice?
—David Livingstone

28. If God's love is for anybody anywhere, it's for everybody everywhere.
—**Edward Lawlor,**
Nazarene General Superintendent

29. If Jesus Christ be God and died for me, then no sacrifice can be too great for me to make for Him.
—**C.T. Studd**

30. If missions languish, it is because the whole life of godliness is feeble. The command to go everywhere and preach to everybody is not obeyed until the will is lost by self-surrender in the will of God.
—**Arthur T. Pierson**

31. If ten men are carrying a log-nine of them on the little end an one at the heavy end—and you want to help, which end will you lift on?
—**William Borden**

32. If the Great Commission is true, our plans are not too big; they are too small.
—**Pat Morley**

33. If we have not enough in our religion . . . to share it with all the world, it is doomed here at home.
—**David Livingstone**

> **If Jesus Christ be God and died for me, then no sacrifice can be too great for me to make for Him.**
>
> —C.T. Studd

34. If you don't have a definite call to stay here, you are called to go.
—**Keith Green**

If you don't have a definite call to stay here, you are called to go.

—Keith Green

35. If you found a cure for cancer, wouldn't it be inconceivable to hide it from the rest of mankind? How much more inconceivable to keep silent the cure from the eternal wages of death.
—Dave Davidson

36. If you take missions out of the Bible, you won't have anything left but the covers.
—Nina Gunter

37. In no other way can the believer become as fully involved with God's work, especially the work of world evangelism, as in intercessory prayer.
—Dick Eastman

38. In our lifetime, wouldn't it be sad if we spent more time washing dishes or swatting flies or mowing the yard or watching television than praying for world missions?
—Dave Davidson

39. In the vast plain to the north I have sometimes seen, in the morning sun, the smoke of a thousand villages where no missionary has ever been.
—Robert Moffat

40. It is possible for the most obscure person in a church, with a heart right toward God, to exercise as much power for the evangelization of the world, as it is for those who stand in the most prominent positions.
—John R. Mott

41. It's better to obey God rather than men.
—Brother Andrew

42. Let my heart be broken with the things that break God's heart.
   —Bob Pierce,
   World Vision founder

43. Life is either a daring adventure, or nothing!
   —Helen Keller
   (She wasn't a missionary, but this is an inspiring mission thought!)

44. Life is precarious, and life is precious. Don't presume you will have it tomorrow, and don't waste it today.
   —John Piper

Lost people matter to God, and so they must matter to us.

—Keith Wright

45. Live God LOUD!
   —Ron Luce

46. Lost people matter to God, and so they must matter to us.
   —Keith Wright

47. Missionary zeal does not grow out of intellectual beliefs, nor out of theological arguments, but out of love.
   —Roland Allen

48. Missions is not just for missionaries; God's call is for all.
   —Jon & Ann Dunagan

49. Missions is not the ultimate goal of the church. Worship is. Missions exists because worship doesn't.
   —John Piper

50. Missions is the overflow of our delight in God because missions is the overflow of God's delight in being God.
—**John Piper**

51. Never pity missionaries; envy them. They are where the real action is—where life and death, sin and grace, Heaven and Hell converge.
—**Robert C. Shannon**

52. No reserves. No retreats. No regrets.
—**William Borden**

53. Not, how much of my money will I give to God, but, how much of God's money will I keep for myself?
—**John Wesley**

54. Oh, that I could spend every moment of my life to God's glory!
—**David Brainerd**

55. Oh, that I had a thousand lives and a thousand bodies! All of them should be devoted to no other employment but to preach Christ to these degraded, despised, yet beloved mortals.
—**Robert Moffat**

56. One Way: Jesus! One Job: Evangelism!
—**T.L. Osborn**

57. Only as the church fulfills her missionary obligation does she justify her existence.
—**Unknown**

58. On the cross, Jesus bled out completely—He held nothing back! In return, God wants you to give everything to Him—to hold nothing back!
—**Jon Dunagan**

59. Our God of Grace often gives us a second chance, but there is no second chance to harvest a ripe crop.
—**Kurt von Schleicher**

60. Some wish to live within the sound of church and chapel bell. I want to run a rescue shop within a yard of hell!
—**C.T. Studd**

61. Someone asked, Will the heathen who have never heard the Gospel be saved? It is more a question with me whether we—who have the Gospel and fail to give it to those who have not—can be saved.
—**Charles Spurgeon**

62. Tell the students to give up their small ambitions and come eastward to preach the Gospel of Christ.
—**Francis Xavier**

63. The best remedy for a sick church is to put it on a missionary diet.
—**David Livingstone**

64. This generation can only reach this generation.
—**David Livingstone**

65. Sympathy is no substitute for action.
—**David Livingstone**

66. The Bible is not the basis of missions; missions is the basis of the Bible.
—**Ralph Winter,**
     U.S. Center for World Mission

67. The Christian is not obedient unless he is doing all in his power to send the Gospel to the heathen world.
—**A. B. Simpson**

68. The Church must send or the church will end.
—**Mendell Taylor**

69. The church that does not evangelize will fossilize.
—**Oswald J. Smith**

70. The mission of the church is missions.
—**Oswald J. Smith**

71. God's mission is for your family to expand His family.
—**Jon & Ann Dunagan**

72. We talk of the Second Coming; half the world has never heard of the first.
—**Oswald J. Smith**

73. The bedrock foundation for our call to world missions is the blood of Jesus Christ.
—**Jon Dunagan**

74. The church which ceases to be evangelistic will soon cease to be evangelical.
—**Alexander Duff**

75. The Gospel is only good news if it gets there in time.
—**Carl F. H. Henry**

76. The Great Commission is not an option to be considered; it is a command to be obeyed.
—**Hudson Taylor**

77. The Great Commission is the Great Adventure of Christianity.
—**Ron Luce, TeenMania**

78. The history of missions is the history of answered prayer.
—**Samuel Zweme**

79. The light that shines farthest shines brightest nearest home.
—**C. T. Studd**

80. The mark of a great church is not its seating capacity, but its sending capacity.
—**Mike Stachura**

81. There is nothing in the world or the Church—except the church's disobedience—to render the evangelization of the world in this generation an impossibility.
—**Robert Speer**

82. The spirit of Christ is the spirit of missions. The nearer we get to Him, the more intensely missionary we become.
—**Henry Martyn,**
        Missionary to India and Persia

83. The supreme task of the Church is the evangelization of the world.
—**Oswald J. Smith**

84. The will of God—nothing less, nothing more, nothing else.
—**F. E. Marsh**
        (also attributed to Bobby Richardson)

85. To know God and to make Him known.
—**Loren Cunningham,**
        YWAM

86. To know the will of God, we need an open Bible and an open map.
—**William Carey**

Untold millions are still untold.

—John Wesley

87. Untold millions are still untold.
—**John Wesley**

88. Walk away from your own preoccupations . . . and see the perishing multitudes.
—**K.P. Yohannan,**
        Gospel for Asia

89. We are debtors to every man to give him the Gospel in the same measure in which we have received it.
—P.F. Bresee

90. We must be global Christians with a global vision because our God is a global God.
—John Stott

91. What can we do to win these men to Christ?
—Richard Wurmbrand,
    The Voice of the Martyrs (referring to the men who were persecuting him)

92. Why should anyone hear the Gospel twice, before everyone has heard it once?
—Oswald J. Smith

93. Will you go to His feet and place yourself entirely at His disposal?
—General William Booth
    The Salvation Army

94. Will you shed your tears for the souls of the nations?
—Wendi Stranz,
    Pastor's wife

95. World missions was on God's mind from the beginning.
—Dave Davidson

96. You can give without loving. But you cannot love without giving.
—Amy Carmichael

97. You can only export what you grow at home.
—Jon Dunagan

98. You can't take it with you, but you can send it on ahead.
—Oswald J. Smith

99. You must go or send a substitute.
—**Oswald J. Smith**

100. You have one business on earth-to save souls.
—**John Wesley**

More Missionary Quotes:

The biggest hindrance to the missionary task is self. Self that refuses to die. Self that refuses to sacrifice. Self that refuses to give.
Self that refuses to go.
—**Thomas Hale,**
Missionary to Nepal

I had utterly abandoned myself to Him. Could any choice be as wonderful as His will? Could any place be safer than the center of His will? Did not he assure me by His very presence that His thoughts toward us are good, and not evil? Death to my own plans and desires was almost deliriously delightful. Everything was laid at His nail-scarred feet, life or death, health or illness, appreciation by others or misunderstanding, success or failure as measured by human standards. Only He himself mattered.
—**V. Raymond Edman**

Believers who have the Gospel keep mumbling it over and over to themselves. Meanwhile, millions who have never heard it once fall into the flames of eternal hell without ever hearing the salvation story.
—**K.P. Yohannan,**
Gospel for Asia

Life is pitiful, death so familiar, suffering and pain so common, yet I would not be anywhere else. Do not wish me out of this or in any way seek to get me out, for I will not be got out while this trial is on. These are my people, God has given them to me, and I will live or die for Him and His glory.
—**Gladys Aylward**

The command has been to "go," but we have stayed — in body, gifts, prayer and influence. He has asked us to be witnesses unto the uttermost parts of the earth . . . but 99% of Christians have kept puttering around in the homeland.
—**Robert Savage**

God is not calling us to win the world and, in the process, lose our families. But I have known those who so enshrined family life and were so protective of "quality time" that the children never saw in their parents the kind of consuming love that made their parent's faith attractive to them. Some have lost their children, not because they weren't at their soccer games or didn't take family vacations, but because they never transmitted a loyalty to Jesus that went deep enough to interrupt personal preferences.
—**David Shibley,**
       The Missions Addiction

'Not called!' did you say? 'Not heard the call,' I think you should say. Put your ear down to the Bible, and hear Him bid you go and pull sinners out of the fire of sin. Put your ear down to the burdened, agonized heart of humanity, and listen to its pitiful wail for help. Go stand by the gates of hell, and hear the damned entreat you to go to their father's house and bid their brothers and sisters and servants and masters not to come there. Then look Christ in the face—whose mercy you have

professed to obey—and tell Him whether you will join heart and soul and body and circumstances in the march to publish His mercy to the world.
—**General William Booth,**
    The Salvation Army

God is pursuing with omnipotent passion a worldwide purpose of gathering joyful worshipers for Himself from every tribe and tongue and people and nation. He has an inexhaustible enthusiasm for the supremacy of His name among the nations. Therefore, let us bring our affections into line with His, and, for the sake of His name, let us renounce the quest for worldly comforts and join His global purpose.
—**John Piper**

All men dream, but not equally. Those who dream by night in the dusty recesses of their minds wake in the day to find that it was vanity. But the dreamers of the day are dangerous men, for they may act their dream with open eyes, to make it possible. This I did.
—**T. E. Lawrence**

The concern for world evangelization is not something tacked on to a man's personal Christianity, which he may take or leave as he chooses. It is rooted in the character of the God who has come to us in Christ Jesus. Thus, it can never be the province of a few enthusiasts, a sideline or a specialty of those who happen to have a bent that way. It is the distinctive mark of being a Christian.
—**James S. Stewart**

God is a God of missions. He wills missions. He commands missions. He demands missions. He made missions possible through His Son. He made missions actual in sending the Holy Spirit.
—**George W. Peters**

**If you take missions
out of the Bible,
you won't have anything
left but the covers.**

—Nina Gunter

8

100 Mission Verses

Nothing but the Blood
from Genesis to Revelation

God's plan to bring His salvation to the whole world- through Christ's saving blood-is a central theme of God's Word. (Note: in this chapter, most verses are condensed for brevity, from the NKJV, unless otherwise noted).

Since the time of Adam and Eve, all people have sinned and all need a Savior.

1. Genesis 2:17
When you eat of its fruit, you will surely die.

2. Genesis 3:6
Eve ate its fruit; Adam ate it also.

3. Psalms 14:3
No one does good, not even one.

4. Romans 5:12
Through one man sin entered the world.

5. Romans 3:10
There is none righteous, no, not one.

From the beginning, God required innocent blood to be shed for the guilty.

6. Revelation 13:8
. . . Lamb slain from the foundation of the world.

7. Genesis 3:21
God made garments of skin for Adam and Eve.

8. Leviticus 17:11
It is the blood that makes atonement.

9. Hebrews 9:22
. . . without shedding of blood there is no remission.

God's Heart for World Missions from Genesis 12:1-3

**Now the LORD had said to Abram:
"Get out of your country, From your family
And from your father's house,
To a land that I will show you.**

**I will make you a great nation;
I will bless you And make your name great;
And you shall be a blessing.**

**I will bless those who bless you,
And I will curse him who curses you;
And in you all the families of the earth
shall be blessed."**

All people descend from Adam and Noah.

10. Acts 17:26
From one man, Adam, God made every nation.

11. Genesis 10:32
From Noah's sons the nations spread over earth.

God is no respecter of persons.

12. Romans 10:12
There is no distinction between Jew and Greek.

13. Acts 10:34-35
God accepts men from any nation who fear Him.

14. James 2:1-9
Be like God–do not show partiality.

God revealed His love for the Gentiles in the Old Testament Law and Passover.

15. Exodus 12:48
Gentiles are invited to celebrate the Passover.

16. Leviticus 16:29
Gentiles can take part in the Day of Atonement.

17. Leviticus 19:10
The people of Israel are encouraged to leave fallen grapes for the poor and for the Gentiles.

18. Leviticus 22:18
Gentiles are permitted to offer sacrifices.

19. Numbers 15:14
Gentiles are given regulations for sacrifices.

God promised blessings through Abraham's descendants for all nations on the earth.

20. Genesis 12:1-3
In you all families of the earth will be blessed.

21. Genesis 18:18
All nations will be blessed through Abraham.

22. Acts 3:25
In Abraham's seed all peoples will be blessed.

Through signs and wonders, many nations heard of God's power and gave Him honor.

23. Exodus 7:5
The Egyptians will know that I am the Lord.

24. Exodus 15:11-14
The nations will hear and tremble.

25. 2 Kings 5:15
There is no God except in Israel . . .

The Old Testament prophets and Psalms revealed God's heart for all nations.

26. Isaiah 45:22-23
Turn to Me and be saved, all you ends of the earth!

27. Jeremiah 1:5
I ordained you a prophet to the nations.

28. Jeremiah 16:19
O Lord, the Gentiles shall come to You.

29. Ezekiel 39:21
I will display My glory among the nations.

30. Joel 3:9-14
Proclaim this among the nations . . .

31. Zechariah 8:20-23
Many peoples and nations will seek the Lord.

Ask of me, and I shall give thee the heathen for thine inheritance, and the uttermost parts of the earth for thy possession.

—Psalm 2:8 (KJV)

32. Psalm 18:49
I will give thanks to You among the Gentiles.

33. Psalm 22:27
All the families of the nations will worship You.

34. Psalm 33:8,12
Let all the people of the world revere Him.

35. Psalm 57:9
I will praise You, O Lord, among the nations.

36. Psalm 67
Oh, let the nations be glad and sing for joy!

37. Psalm 96:2-3
Declare His glory among the nations.

38. Psalm 117
Praise the Lord, all you Gentiles.

God was glorified in the sight of other nations through Old Testament leaders and characters.

39. Genesis 45:8
God lifted up Joseph before Pharaoh.

40. Exodus 7:5
God showed His power in Egypt through Moses.

41. I Kings 10:1-9
Queen of Sheba saw God's wisdom in Solomon.

42. Daniel 3:28
Example of Shadrach, Meshach, and Abednego.

43. Daniel 6:25-27
All commanded to fear God because of Daniel.

Old Testament Gentiles who had faith in God were saved.

44. Joshua 2:8-21
Rahab, a sinful woman, is saved at Jericho.

45. Ruth 4; Matt. 1:5
Ruth, a woman of Moab, joins Jesus' lineage.

46. Jonah 4:2
The wicked city of Nineveh is saved.

47. I Kings 17:7-24
God provides for a Gentile widow.

48. 2 Kings 5
Namaan, a Syrian captain, is healed of leprosy.

Through Jesus Christ's birth, God proclaimed His salvation for all people.

49. Matthew 2:1-12
Wise men from the East come to worship Jesus.

50. Luke 2:8-14
(Angel to shepherds) I bring you good tidings of great joy which will be to all people . . .

51. Luke 2:27-32
(Simeon's prophesy over baby Jesus)
. . . So he came by the Spirit into the temple. And when the parents brought in the Child Jesus, to do for Him according to the custom of the law, he took Him up in his arms and blessed God and said: "Lord, now You are letting Your servant depart in peace, According to Your word; For my eyes have seen Your salvation. Which You have prepared before the face of all peoples, A light to bring revelation to the Gentiles, And the glory of Your people Israel."

Through His ministry and preaching, Jesus demonstrated God's heart for all people.

52. Luke 4:25-27
Jesus' first sermon lauds two Gentiles.

53. Luke 8:26-37
A Gentile man is set free from demons.

54. John 4:1-26
Jesus offers a Samaritan woman "living water."

55. Matthew 8:5-13
Jesus affirms a Roman centurion's "great faith."

In His final words (recorded in all four Gospels and in Acts), Jesus gave His Great Commission.

56. Matthew 28:19
Go and make disciples of all the nations.

57. Mark 16:15
Go into all the world and preach the Gospel.

58. Luke 24:47
Repentance will be preached to all nations.

59. John 20:21
As the Father has sent Me, I also send you.

60. Acts 1:8
You will be My witnesses to the end of the earth.

When Jesus died, His blood was shed for all people on earth. Only through His blood can people be saved.

61. John 1:12
. . . as many as received Him . . .

62. John 3:16
Whoever believes in Him shall not perish.

63. John 1:29
(John the Baptist to Jesus)
Behold! The Lamb of God who takes away the sin of the world!

64. Colossians 1:19-20
God has made peace through Christ's blood.

65. Revelation 5:9
You have redeemed us by Your blood.

Jesus Christ is the only way to heaven.

66. John 14:6
No one comes to the Father except through Me.

67. John 3:1-7
You must be born again.

68. John 3:18
He who does not believe is condemned already.

69. Acts 4:12
No other name by which we must be saved.

Without Jesus, the heathen are lost, separated from God, and will spend eternity in hell.

70. Proverbs 15:11
Hell and destruction are before the Lord.

71. Mark 9:42-47
Jesus' warnings about sin, and hell fire.

72. Romans 3:23
All have sinned and fall short of God's glory.

73. Romans 6:23
For the wages of sin is death, but the gift of God is eternal life in Christ Jesus our Lord.

74. Romans 10:14-15
And how shall they believe in Him of whom they have not heard? . . . "How beautiful are the feet of those who preach the Gospel of peace..."

75. Galatians 5:19-21
Those who practice such things (the works of the flesh) will not inherit the kingdom of God.

God places in all people knowledge of God their Creator and a consciousness of sin, so that all are without excuse.

76. Ecclesiastes 3:11
God has put eternity in their hearts.

77. Psalm 19:1-3
The heavens declare the glory of God; And the firmament shows His handiwork. Day unto day utters speech, And night unto night reveals knowledge. There is no speech nor language Where their voice is not heard.

78. John 1:9
That was the true Light which gives light to every man coming into the world.

79. Romans 1:18-20
God's attributes are clear; we are without excuse.

It is God's desire for everyone to be saved.

80. Ezekiel 33:11
I take no pleasure in the death of the wicked.

81. John 3:16
For God so loved the world that He gave His only begotten Son, that whoever believes in Him should not perish but have everlasting life.

82. John 3:17
For God did not send His Son into the world to condemn the world, but that the world through Him might be saved.

83. 2 Peter 3:9
The Lord is . . . not willing that any should perish but that all should come to repentance.

84. Romans 10:13
For "whoever calls on the name of the Lord shall be saved."

The early church believers were active in missionary work among other people groups.

85. Acts 8:4-6
Philip went to preach in Samaria.

86. Acts 8:26-39
God led Philip to an Ethiopian.

87. Acts 10
God led Peter to Cornelius and fellow Gentiles.

88. Acts 10:34-35
Then Peter opened his mouth and said: "In truth I perceive that God shows no partiality. But in every nation whoever fears Him and works righteousness is accepted by Him.

89. Acts 16:9-10
Paul's "Macedonian call"

90. Romans 1:16
For I am not ashamed of the Gospel of Christ, for it is the power of God to salvation for everyone who believes, for the Jew first and also for the Greek.

91. II Corinthians 10:16
. . . to preach the Gospel in the regions beyond you . . .

In the Bible, the world is referred to as a field "ripe for harvest." We must reap these souls now, before they are lost.

92. Proverbs 10:5
He who gathers in summer is a wise son; He who sleeps in harvest is a son who causes shame.

93. Joel 3:13-14
Put in the sickle, for the harvest is ripe. Come, go down; For the winepress is full, The vats overflow—For their wickedness is great." Multitudes, multitudes in the valley of decision! For the day of the Lord is near in the valley of decision.

94. Matthew 9:37-38
Then He said to His disciples, "The harvest truly is plentiful, but the laborers are few. Therefore pray the Lord of the harvest to send out laborers into His harvest."

95. Luke 10:2
Then He said to them, "The harvest truly is great, but the laborers are few; therefore pray the Lord of the harvest to send out laborers into His harvest.

96. John 4:34-36
Jesus said to them, "My food is to do the will
of Him who sent Me, and to finish His work.
Do you not say, 'There are still four months and
then comes the harvest'? Behold, I say to you,
lift up your eyes and look at the fields, for they
are already white for harvest! And he who reaps
receives wages, and gathers fruit for eternal life,
that both he who sows and he who reaps may
rejoice together.

In Revelation, all tribes, tongues, peoples, and nations worship the Lamb.

97. Revelation 5:9
And have redeemed us to God by Your blood Out
of every tribe and tongue and people . . .

98. Revelation 7:9-10
a great multitude from every nation, tribe . . .

99. Revelation 14:6
the eternal Gospel to preach to every nation. . .

100. Revelation 21:24
The nations will walk by its light.

God's Heart for World Missions
from Revelation 5:8-9

Now when He had taken the scroll, the
four living creatures and the twenty-four
elders fell down before the Lamb,
each having a harp, and golden bowls
full of incense, which are the
prayers of the saints.

And they sang a new song, saying:
"You are worthy to take the scroll, And to
open its seals; For You were slain, And
have redeemed us to God by Your blood,
Out of every tribe and tongue
and people and nation..."

**And they overcame him
by the blood of the Lamb,
and by the word
of their testimony: and
they loved not their lives
unto the death.**

—Revelation 12:11

9

100 Missionary Martyrs
Remembering Those Who Gave Their All

Imagine walking over a rolling hillside of a cemetery dedicated to the lives of missionaries and martyrs throughout history—both of Christian heroes who were *killed* for their faith, and also of godly men and women who sacrificially *lived* their lives by "giving their all" for God's purposes. Just reading the names, dates, and ministry summaries of these believers would be challenging and inspiring.

Over the years, our family has visited several military cemeteries and war memorials. Not to equate military heroes with Christian martyrs; but as we have walked past row after row of grave-side crosses, with name after name of unknown soldiers, it has been thought-provoking to consider all the lives that have been dedicated to a common cause or a country. We have noticed that most of the graves mark the lives of the common foot soldiers, with only a few of the larger headstones commemorating the officers and generals; yet every cross and every life represented marks a complete sacrifice. Together, their graves give a testimony to the vision for which they died.

> **"Don't waste your life."**
>
> —John Piper

"from these honored dead ... "

In 1863, as President Abraham Lincoln dedicated the battlefield cemetery at Gettysburg (during the Civil War), his words echoed a timeless challenge:

> ". . . that from these honored dead we take increased devotion to that cause for which they gave the last full measure of devotion—that we here highly resolve that these dead shall not have died in vain."

As Christian believers, how much more should we ponder the lives and devotion of godly martyrs and missionaries who gave their lives for God's eternal cause and kingdom? We don't just serve a president or an earthly commander; we serve the King of kings and the Lord of lords; and He led the way, by willingly dying for us.

C.T. Studd, a missionary to India, Africa, and China, who recruited hundreds of other missionaries, said:

> "If Jesus Christ be God and died for me,
> then no sacrifice can be too great
> for me to make for Him."

The blood of the martyrs is the seed:

Tertullian, a second-century church leader said, "The blood of the martyrs is the seed of Christians."

Throughout biblical and Christian history, the willing sacrifice of the martyrs has been a "seed" which has led to the conversion of many believers.

"We died before we came ... "

When James Calvert (1813-1892) went out as a missionary to the cannibals of the Fiji Islands, the ship captain tried to turn him back saying,

"You will lose your life and the lives of those with you if you go among such savages."

To that, Calvert replied,

"We died before we came here."

In another example, Betty Scott Stam (1906-1934) felt called to become a missionary to China during a difficult and dangerous time—amid news of Communist threats, uprisings, and hardships due to the Great Depression.

Yet long before leaving for China (where she and her husband, John Stam, faithfully served as Christian missionaries and where they were eventually martyred), she had already surrendered everything to God. In her prayer journal, she wrote:

Lord, I give up
All my own plans and purposes,
All my own desires and hopes, and accept
Thy will for my life.

I give myself, my life, my all, utterly to Thee
To be Thine forever.
Fill me and seal me with Thy Holy Spirit.
Use me as Thou wilt. Send me where Thou wilt.
Work out Thy whole will in my life
At any cost, Now and forever.

—Betty Scott Stam

But the "point" of the Christian life is not merely *to go and die* as martyrs, but rather, *to live* for Christ-to fully live for God's purposes.

And a completely surrendered and submitted life should not be considered extraordinary. In the Bible, it is merely our "reasonable" service:

> "I beseech you therefore, brethren, by the
> mercies of God, that you present your bodies
> a living sacrifice, holy, acceptable to God,
> which is your reasonable service.
> —Romans 12:1

> Does he thank that servant because
> he did the things that were commanded him?
> I think not.
> So likewise you, when you have done all those
> things which you are commanded, say,
> "We are unprofitable servants.
> We have done what was our duty to do."'
> —Luke 17:9-10

> And those who are Christ's
> have crucified the flesh
> with its passions and desires.
> If we live in the Spirit,
> let us also walk in the Spirit.
> —Galations 5:24-25

(Note: How many of us are called to crucify the flesh with its passions and desires? It's a call for ALL of us—ALL "those who are Christ's . . . ")

100 Who Gave Their All for Jesus:

The Twelve Apostles

1. James (died in 44 AD)-First of the twelve apostles to be martyred for his faith. The Bible records how he was seized by King Herod and killed with a sword (see Acts 12:1-2).

2. **Peter** (1 BC - 67 AD)-Established the church in Antioch and preached to the Gentiles. Martyred by being crucified upside-down ("not worthy to be crucified in the same way as his Savior").

3. **John** (6-100 AD)—Author of the Gospel of John, I-II-III John, and Revelation. Tradition says he was imprisoned for his faith, and plunged into boiling oil (yet that did not kill him). John was banished to the Island of Patmos, and he died of old age.

4. **Philip** (died in 80 AD)-Preached in Greece, Syria, and Phrygia (modern-day Turkey). Martyred by being crucified upside-down. From his cross, he continued to preach the Gospel, until his death.

5. **Andrew** (died in mid-late 1st century AD)—Preached in Asia minor, along the Black Sea (as far as the Volga and Kiev, becoming known as the "patron saint" of Russia, Ukraine, and Romania). Martyred by being crucified on an X-shaped cross.

6. **Matthew** (died in the 1st century AD)—Preached to the Jews, Macedonians, Persians, Parthians, and Ethiopians (of Egyptian descent), and was martyred.

7. **Bartholomew**, also called Nathanael (died in the 1st century AD)—Tradition says he preached the Gospel in India and in Armenia. He was martyred by being flayed alive, and then crucified head-down.

8. **Thomas** (died in 72 AD)-Perhaps the only apostle who brought the Gospel of Jesus Christ outside of the Roman Empire. Preached the Gospel in

the Parthian Empire and in India (where he was martyred).

9. **James**, known as James the Son of Alphaeus (died in the 1st century AD)—Preached the Gospel in Egypt. Martyred by being beaten with a club and then beheaded.

10. **Thaddeus**, also called Jude (died about 65 AD)—Preached the Gospel in Judea, Samaria, Idumaea, Syria, Mesopotamia, and Libya. Martyred in Beirut.

11. **Simon**, known as Simon the Zealot. (died in the 1st century AD)—Preached in the Middle East and Africa. According to legend, was martyred by being sawn in half.

12. **Matthias**, the apostle who replaced Judas (died in 80 AD)—Preached in an area which is now known as the modern-day country of Georgia (in Eurasia). Martyred in Jerusalem by being stoned and then beheaded.

Other Martyrs of the Early Church

13. **Stephen** (died in 34 AD)—Martyred by being stoned to death for preaching the Gospel (see Acts 6).

14. **Barnabas** (died in 61 AD)—Evangelized the Gentiles with Paul. While preaching the Gospel in Cyprus, he was dragged out of the synagogue, tortured, and stoned to death.

15. **Paul** (5 - 67 AD)—Preached the Gospel around the Mediterranean, wrote much of the New Testament. Was shipwrecked and imprisoned. Beheaded during the reign of Nero, in Rome.

16. **Mark** (died in 68 AD)-Honored as the founder of Christianity in Africa. While preaching in

Alexandria, a rope was placed around his neck, and he was dragged through the city, until dead.

17. **Luke** (died in 84 AD)-Wrote the Gospel of Luke. Ministered with Paul throughout various countries and according to tradition, was martyred by being hung on an olive tree by idolatrous priests in Greece.

18. **Ignatius** (35 - 107 AD)—Early Christian Martyr. Was thrown to the lions and eaten alive. "I would rather die for Christ than rule the whole earth."—Ignatius

19. **Polycarp** (69 - 155 AD)—Last Christian leader to know the original apostles. Was thrown into a fire, but according to tradition, his body would not burn. Finally martyred by being killed with a sword by soldiers, who then burned his body.

20. **Perpetua** (died in 203 AD)—A young 22-year-old noblewoman and nursing mother who died for Christ. She was martyred in the Carthage arena (in the Roman province of Africa) by being tortured by a wild cow and finally killed by a gladiator (along with co-martyr, **Felicity**, an expectant mother).

The "Holy Forty"

21 - 61. The "Holy Forty" (died in 320 AD). Also known as **"The Forty Martyrs of Sebaste."**

During the persecutions of Licinius (who after 316 AD persecuted Christians of the East), forty Roman soldiers, in the group "Legio XII Fulminata" (meaning "Armed with Lightning") openly professed their faith in Jesus Christ.

Because of their Christian confession, these forty men were condemned to be martyred by being exposed naked on a frozen pond near Sebaste (in an area called "Lesser Armenia"), that they might freeze to death.

According to Bishop Basil of Caesarea (370-379), who commemorated their martyrdom, here is the account:

Among those who confessed Christ, one sadly yielded and, leaving his companions, sought the warm baths near the lake which had been prepared for any who might turn back and deny their faith.

One of the guards who kept watch over the martyrs saw at this moment a supernatural brilliancy overshadowing them and at once proclaimed himself a Christian, threw off his garments, and joined the remaining thirty-nine.

Thus the number of forty remained complete.

At daybreak, the stiffened bodies of the confessors, which still showed signs of life, were burned and the ashes cast into a river.

62. Valentine (died around 269)—Throughout the time of ancient Rome, several Christian believers (14 in all) named "Valentine" were martyred for their faith. St. Valentine's Day is named in their honor.

63. Patrick (386-461)—Missionary to Ireland who converted thousands of people from pagan beliefs to faith in Jesus Christ. St. Patrick's Day is named in his honor.

64. John Wycliffe (1320 - 1384)—Preacher and Bible Translator. He died of a stroke in 1384. In 1415, a counsel declared him a heretic of the church; his books were burned; and his remains were dug-up, burned, and his ashes thrown in the Swift River.

65. John Huss (1369 - 1415)—Early Reformer of the Middle Ages. Martyred by being burned at a stake.

66. Martin Luther (1483-1546)—Reformation Leader and Bible Translator.

67. David Brainerd (1718 - 1747)—American missionary evangelist to the Native Americans.

> Oh, that I could spend every moment
> of my life to God's glory!

> All my desire was the conversion of the
> heathen, and all my hope was in God

> —David Brainerd

68. Count Nicolaus Ludwig von Zinzendorf (1700-1760)—Founder of the Moravian Church (which focused on single-mindedness, identification with Jesus Christ and world evangelism). The Moravians began a prayer vigil in 1727, which continued, 24-hours a day, seven days a week, uninterrupted, for over 100 years.

69. William Carey (1761-1834)—Missionary to India and Bible translator. Throughout 42 years in ministry, William Carey and his coworkers translated the entire Bible into 26 languages, and the New Testament into 25 more. Known as the Father of Modern Missions.

70. & 71. Marcus Whitman (1802 - 1847) **& Narcissa Whitman** (1808 - 1847)—American Pioneer Missionaries to the Oregon Territory. Both martyred.

72. David Livingstone (1813 - 1873)—Great missionary explorer to Africa.

73. Dr. Alexander Duff (1806-1878)—Missionary from Scotland to India.

"Dr. Duff's Appeal

from *The Challenge of Missions:*

Dr. Alexander Duff, that great veteran missionary to India, returned to Scotland to die, and as he stood before the General Assembly of the Presbyterian Church, he made his appeal, but there was no response.

In the midst of his appeal he fainted and was carried off the platform. The doctor bent over him and examined his heart.

Presently he opened his eyes. "Where am I?" he cried. "Where am I?"

"Lie still," said the doctor, "You have had a heart attack. Lie still."

But in spite of the protests of the physician, the old warrior struggled to his feet, and, with the doctor on one side and the moderator of the assembly on the other side, he again mounted the steps of the pulpit platform. As he did so, the entire assembly rose to do him honor. Then, when they were seated, he continued with his appeal. And this is what he said:

"When Queen Victoria calls for volunteers for India, hundreds of young men respond; but, when King Jesus calls, no one goes." Then he paused. There was silence. Again he spoke:

"Very well," he concluded, "then, aged though I am, I'll go back to India. I can lie down on the banks of the Ganges and I can die and thereby I can let the people of India know that there was one man in Scotland who loved them enough to give his life for them."

In a moment, young men all over the assembly sprang to their feet, crying, "I'll go! I'll go!"

And after the old white-haired warrior had been laid to rest, these young men, having graduated, found their way to dark benighted India, there to labor as his substitutes for the Lord Jesus Christ.

My friend, will you go? Has God spoken to you? Have you heard His Call?

Will you not answer, "Lord, here am I, send me"? And if you cannot go, will you not send a substitute? It is for you to decide. Why should anyone hear the Gospel twice before everyone has heard it once?

74. Charles (Carl) Lwanga (1860 - 1886)—One of many martyrs in Uganda, Christians (Roman Catholics and Anglicans) who were murdered by Mwanga II, the Kabaka (King) of Buganda, between 1885 and 1887.

75. James Calvert (1813 - 1892)—Wesleyan Methodist Missionary from England to Fiji. See excerpt page 115.

76. George Müller (1805 - 1898)—Known as a man of prayer and faith, caring for over 120,000 orphans in Bristol, England (without asking for money), and traveling over 200,000 miles (by ship) throughout the world, preaching about world missions and trusting in God.

77. Hudson Taylor (1832 - 1905)—Missionary to China and founder of the China Island Mission. Great missionary patriarch, known as a man of mission and a man of prayer.

78. & 79. General William Booth (1829-1912)—**& Catherine Booth** (1829-1890)-Founders of the Salvation Army and faithful to their family. See writing excerpt on pp. 142-151.

80. Lottie Moon (1840 - 1912)-Missionary to China, faithfully ministering for 39 years. During a time of war and famine, despite many requests for help, Moon died of starvation on a boat docked in Japan - on Christmas Eve.

81. Mary Slessor (1848 - 1915)—African Missionary. She went to Africa as a young woman, and spent her life as a missionary. She died in a simple mud hut.

82. & 83. John Stam (1907 - 1934)-**& Betty Scott Stam** (1906-1934)-Both martyred in China. See Betty Stam's prayer on page 115.

84. Eric Liddell (1902 - 1945)-Olympic Gold Medalist from Scotland and missionary to China (died in a Japanese prison camp shortly before the end of WWII).

85. Amy Carmichael (1867 - 1951)—Missionary to India - Rescued hundreds of children from Hindu temple prostitution. See writing excerpt on pp. 132-138.

A Communist officer told a Christian he was beating, "I am almighty, as you suppose your God to be. I can kill you."

The Christian answered, "The power is all on my side. I can love you while you torture me to death."

—Jesus Freaks, by dc Talk and
The Voice of the Martyrs

Five Missionary Martyrs in Ecuador:

In 1956, five young missionary men were martyred in Ecuador while bringing the gospel to the remote "Auca" tribe (now known as the Huaorani people). Many books, magazine articles, and films have documented their lives, and many Christians have been inspired by their sacrificial devotion to Christ:

"He is no fool who gives up what he cannot
keep to gain that which he cannot lose."

—Jim Elliot

86. Jim Elliot
87. Nate Saint
88. Pete Fleming
89. Ed McCully
90. Roger Youderian

People who do not know the Lord ask why in the world we waste our lives as missionaries.

They forget that they too are expending their lives . . .
and when the bubble has burst, they will have nothing of eternal significance to show for the years they have wasted.

—Nate Saint

91. Gladys Aylward (1902-1970)—Although rejected by mission organizations, Gladys Alyward became a missionary to China. She preached the Gospel and rescued many orphan children during a time of war.

"Life is pitiful, death so familiar, suffering and pain so common, yet I would not be anywhere else. Do not wish me out of this or in any way seek to get me out, for I will not be got out while this trial is on. These are my people, God has given them to me, and I will live or die with them, for Him and His glory."
—Gladys Aylward

92. Watchman Nee (1903-1972)—Chinese martyr, Christian author, and church leader. Honored by Christianity Today as one of the 100 most influential Christians of the twentieth century. In 1952, Nee was imprisoned for his faith, and he died in 1972 in a labor camp. His books are banned in China.

93. William Cameron Townsend (1896-1982)— Founder of Wycliffe Bible Translators

94. Oswald J. Smith (1889-1986)—Missionary Evangelist, spokesman, and author of *The Challenge of Missions*. See writing excerpt on pp. 139-141.

95. Rachel Saint (1914-1994)-Wycliffe Bible Translators in Peru and Ecuador.

96. Richard Wurmbrand (1909-2001)—Tortured and imprisoned for his faith in Romania, for a total of 15 years. Founder of The Voice of the Martyrs. Author of *Tortured for Christ*.

97. Bill Bright (1921-2003)—Founded Campus Crusade for Christ. Author of The Four Spiritual Laws. Received a vision for the JESUS Film, now translated into over 1000 languages.

98. Example of a contemporary Chinese martyr:

Jiang Zongxiu is just one example from the multitudes of today's "unknown" contemporary Christian believers who have been martyred or persecuted for Jesus Christ.

Jiang, age 34, was martyred in 2004. Voice of China Network produced a video documenting how she was arrested for giving Christian Gospel tracts in a local market in Guizhou Province. She was beaten to death the next day while in police custody.

99. Example of a national missionary (and martyr):

"The Man in the Clouds"
-A JESUS Film Testimony:

Several years ago in India, a young national missionary couple felt the call of God to take the Gospel to a very resistant area in the north. They went with their three-year-old son to live among the Maltos people in a notorious area known as the "graveyard of missionaries."

They labored faithfully for many years without seeing a single person come to Christ. Their every effort to share the Gospel was met with opposition. They battled discouragement, depression, spiritual oppression, and polluted water. Often, the entire family was ill.

One day the husband was returning home after seeing the doctor for his severe pain. As he walked through the door of their tiny home he collapsed and died. Distraught, his wife went to check on their sick child. He also had died. Devastated, confused, and with an acute sense of loss, she returned home, seemingly defeated.

A few weeks a later, a JESUS film team arrived in that exact Maltos area. This time the government officials cooperated. The governor had previewed JESUS and instructed that the film be shown and not resisted.

Now, if you have seen JESUS, you know there is a moving scene when Jesus is first revealed at His baptism in the Jordon River. The moment Jesus' face appeared on the screen the crowd erupted with shouts and exclamations. The team had no choice but to stop the film and learn what the commotion was about.

"It's Him, it's Him!" they shouted. They could not believe what they were all seeing. "He is the One we saw walking in the clouds!" The team was astonished at their testimony. It seemed that everyone had seen Him.

It happened the day the national missionary and his son died. Clouds formed over the hillsides. The vision of a man, larger-than-life, appeared above the clouds, walking over their hills, shedding tears.

The Maltos people suspected that it was a message from God, that He was displeased that they had rejected the Gospel. Now, they were being given a second chance. They were stunned. As the team restarted the projector, the people settled down to continue watching the film. Everyone was transfixed by the story. Then, at the end, the majority of these hard, resistance Maltos people put their faith in Christ.

Other miracles followed. People were delivered from evil spirits. The sick were healed. The deep spiritual hunger of many was met.

But the greater miracle is this: where once there were no Christians, there are now 46,000 Maltos believers and hundreds of growing and maturing churches! Today, they are preparing to send out their own missionaries to other unreached people, some of whom will use the JESUS film.

The "graveyard of missionaries" has become the "vineyard of missionaries."

100. This space is reserved for **YOU** to live for Christ:
In the Strong's Concordance, the definition of the
word "martyr" is "a witness."

May you live your life, fully, as a willing sacrifice
and witness for Jesus!

> "We die daily.
> Happy those who daily
> come to life as well."

—George MacDonald

**I have been crucified
with Christ,
nevertheless I live,
yet not I but Christ
who lives in me,
and the life which
I now live in the flesh,
I live by faith
in the Son of God
who loved me and
gave himself for me.**

—Galatians 2:20

Give me the love
that leads the way,
The faith that
nothing can dismay,
The hope no
disappointments tire,
The passion that will
burn like fire.

—Amy Carmichael

The Blood of the Lost

Classic Missionary Stories

- Thy Brother's Blood, by Amy Carmichael
- The Whole Estate, by Oswald J. Smith
- The Fishless Fisherman, by John Drescher
- Who Cares?, by General William Booth

An Introduction to Thy Brother's Blood

Thy Brother's Blood, by Amy Carmichael, is as a compelling vision about the urgent need to share the Gospel with people who are lost. This classic missionary excerpt emphasizes how many believers are distracted by "busy" activities, even in the church (described in the vision as making "daisy chains").

Some Christians view Thy Brother's Blood as overly condemning and "strong"; however, since we first heard it many years ago, read aloud in our World Missions class at Bible college, it has impacted and deepened our perspective and passion for soulwinning.

As you read these compelling words, ask God to challenge your heart about the eternal plight of the lost, and to refresh your priorities. Spiritually, may you begin to see this waterfall of souls—these people who desperately need God's salvation.

Ezekiel 3:18-19 says, "When I say to the wicked, 'You shall surely die, and you give him no warning, nor speak to warn the wicked from his wicked way to save his life, that same wicked man shall die in his iniquity; but his blood I will require at your hand. Yet, if you warn the wicked, and he does not turn from his wickedness, nor from his wicked way, he shall die in his iniquity but you have delivered your soul."

These verses from Ezekiel emphasize the principle of a believer's obligation to warn the wicked of their sin. As Christians, God has called us to share the Gospel with the lost. It is a part of our Great Commandment (to love God and love others) and our Great Commission.

Amy Carmichael:

Amy Carmicael (1867-1951) lived what she believed. For 55 years, she sacrificially served and ministered in India, without a furlough. She is best remembered for her life work of rescuing hundreds of children (especially many girls from Hindu temple prostitution). Other Christians were inspired to join with her, and together with these co-workers, she established a mission called "The Dohnaver Fellowship." Through her books and writings, the impact of Amy Carmichael's life continues to challenge many to a deeper walk with the Lord and a stronger commitment to His service.

Thy Brother's Blood
A Vision of Lost Souls, by Amy Carmichael

The tom-toms thumped straight on all night, and the darkness shuddered 'round me like a living, feeling thing. I could not go to sleep, so I lay awake and looked; and I saw, as it seemed, this . . .

That I stood on a grassy precipice, and at my feet at crevice broke down into infinite space. I looked, but saw no bottom; only cloud shapes, black and furiously coiled, and great shadow-shrouded hollows, and unfathomable depths. Back I drew, dizzy at the depth.

Then I saw forms of people moving in single file along the grass. They were making for the edge.

There was a woman with a baby in her arms and another little child holding onto her dress. She was on the very verge . . .

Then I saw that she was blind. She lifted her foot for the next step . . . it trod air. She was over, and the children over with her. Oh, the cry as they went over!

All were blind, stone blind; and all made straight for the crevice's edge.

Then I saw more streams of people flowing from all quarters. All were blind, stone blind; and all made straight for the crevice's edge. There were shrieks as they suddenly knew in themselves that they were falling, and a tossing up of helpless arms, catching, clutching at empty air. But some went over quietly and fell without a sound.

131

And the green grass seemed blood-red to me, and the gulf yawned like the mouth of hell . . .

Then I wondered with a wonder that was simply agony, why no one stopped them at the edge.

I could not; I was glued to the ground. And I could not call; though I strained and tried, only a whisper would come.

Then I saw that along the edge there were guards set at intervals. But the intervals were too great; there were wide, unguarded gaps between. And over these gaps the people fell in their blindness, quite unwarned; and the green grass seemed blood-red to me, and the gulf yawned like the mouth of hell.

Then I saw, like a little picture of peace, a group of people under some trees with their backs turned towards the gulf. They were making daisy chains . . .

Sometimes when a piercing shriek cut the quiet air and reached them, it disturbed them and they thought it a rather vulgar noise. And if one of their number started up and wanted to go and do something to help, then all the others would pull that one down.

"Why should you get all excited about it? You must wait for a definite call to go! You haven't finished your daisy chain yet. It would be really selfish," they said, "to leave us to finish the work alone."

There was another group. It was made up of people whose great desire was to get more guards out; but they found that very few wanted to go, and sometimes there were no guards set for miles and miles of the edge.

One girl stood alone in her place, waving the people back; but her mother and other relations called, and reminded her that her furlough was due; she must not break the rules.

And being tired and needing a change, she had to go and rest for a while; but no one was sent to guard her gap, and over and over the people fell, like a waterfall of souls.

. . . but no one was sent to guard her gap, and over and over the people fell, like a waterfall of souls.

Once a child caught at a tuft of grass that grew at the very brink of the gulf; it clung convulsively, and it called—but nobody seemed to hear.

Then the roots of the grass gave way, and with a cry the child went over, the two little hands still holding right to the torn-off bunch of grass.

And the girl who longed to be back in her gap thought she heard the little one cry, and she sprang up and wanted to go; at which they reproved her, reminding her that no one is necessary anywhere; the gap would be well taken care of, they knew.

And then they sang a hymn.

Then through the hymn came another sound like the pain of a million broken hearts wrung out in one full drop, one sob.

And a horror of great darkness was upon me, for I knew what it was; the cry of the blood.

And a horror of great darkness was upon me, for I knew what it was; the cry of the blood.

Then thundered a voice, the voice of the Lord. And He said, "What hast thou done? The voice of thy brother's blood crieth unto Me from the ground."

The tom-toms still beat heavily, and darkness still shuddered and shivered about me.

I heard the yells of the devil-dancers and weird, wild shrieks of the devil-possessed just outside the gate.

What does it matter, after all? It has gone on for years; it will go on for years. Why make such a fuss about it?

—God forgive us! God arouse us! Shame us out of our callousness! Shame us out of our sin!

An Introduction to The Whole Estate:

"He who gathers in summer is a wise son; he who sleeps in harvest is a son who causes shame."

—Proverbs 10:5

The Whole Estate, by Oswald J. Smith, focuses on God's call to "the harvest." Growing up on a farm, I (Jon) learned the importance of hard work during harvest time. It was not commendable or exceptional behavior to help bring in the baled hay; it was expected. We all helped and each person's part (whether working in the fields or cooking in the kitchen) was an "obligation" as a member of the family. Unless everyone worked hard, the hay bales could get caught in the rain, and the entire harvest would be damaged or lost. It was not a time to relax. Everyone was needed! As members of God's family, we are also expected to do our part to bring in the world's harvest of souls.

> "Then He said to His disciples, 'The harvest
> truly is plentiful, but the laborers are few.
> Therefore pray the Lord of the harvest to
> send out laborers into His harvest.'"

> —Matthew 9:37-38

Who was Oswald J. Smith?

Oswald J. Smith (1914-1994) was a missionary evangelist, author of *The Challenge of Missions*, a pastor of a mission-oriented church in Canada, and a spokesman for international missions.

The Whole Estate
A Mission Challenge, by Oswald J. Smith

Here is an estate. The master tells his servants that he is leaving, but that He will be returning. And while he is gone, they are to bring the entire estate under cultivation.

They begin working around the house. They beautify the gardens and flowerbeds. Next year the weeds grow and again they go to work, keeping the lawns in perfect condition.

Presently one of them remembers his master's orders. "I must go," he explains. "Our master told us to bring the entire estate under cultivation." And he prepares to leave.

"But," they cry, "we cannot spare you. See how fast the weeds grow. We need you here."

And while he is gone, they are to bring the entire estate under cultivation.

In spite of their protests, however, he leaves and begins working in a far corner of the estate. Later on, two others remember their Lord's orders and in spite of objections they too, go and cultivate another part of the estate.

At last their master returns. He is pleased as he looks at the flowerbeds and gardens and the lawns around his house.

But before rewarding his servants, he decides to explore the rest of the estate and as he does so, his heart sinks for he sees nothing but wilderness and marsh, and he realizes that there has not even been an attempt to cultivate.

. . . and as he does so, his heart sinks for he sees nothing but wilderness and marsh . . .

Finally he comes to the one man working all by himself in a distant part of the estate and he rewards him richly. He discovers the two in still another part and likewise rewards them.

Then he returns to headquarters where his servants are waiting and expecting a reward, but his face indicates displeasure. "Have we not been faithful?" they explain. "Look at these flowerbeds and gardens. Look at these lawns. Are they not beautiful? And have not we worked hard?"

"Yes," he replies, "you have done your best. You have been faithful. You have labored diligently."

"Well then," they cry, "why are you disappointed? Are we not entitled to a reward?"

"There is one thing you have forgotten," he replied. "You have forsaken my orders. I did not tell you to work the same gardens and lawns again and again, year after year. I told you to bring the entire estate under cultivation, to cultivate it, and when your companions insisted upon going and doing their part, you objected. No, there is no reward."

An Intoduction to Who Cares?

Who Cares?, by General William Booth, is a compelling call to reach the lost, presented as a vision of multitudes of people drowning in a rough sea, with many Christians being "distracted" on a rock of safety, and not caring about the others.

This classic mission vision has impacted many Christians for world missions. Written in the 1800s, this old-style of English writing is difficult to read, with long sentences and outdated wording. Yet the message is powerful and the challenge is timeless.

Christian songwriter, Keith Green (who died in 1982), adapted this vision into a modern call to reach the lost, in his song called "Asleep in the Light."

"Do you see, do you see
All the people sinking down
Don't you care, don't you care
Are you gonna let them drown
How can you be so numb
Not to care if they drown
You close your eyes
And pretend the job's done."

General William Booth:

William (1829-1912) and Catherine (1829-1890) Booth founded The Salvation Army, and devoted their lives to reaching the lost. ("General" was a title used by the Salvation Army, not an official military title.) On their banners hung the words "blood and fire" as they fulfilled their mission to "Go for souls, and go for the worst."

Who Cares?
A Vision of Lost Souls, by William Booth, Founder of The Salvation Army

During one of my recent journeys I was led out into a train of thought respecting the conditions of the multitudes around me living regardless of all that concerned their eternal welfare, and in the most open and shameless rebellion against God.

I looked out upon the millions of people around me given up to their drink and their pleasure, and their dancing and their music, and their business and their anxieties, and their politics and their troubles, and thousands of other things; ignorant-willfully ignorant, in many cases: in other instances knowing all about it; but all of them sweeping on and up, in their blasphemies and devilries, to the Throne of God; and while thus musing I had a vision . . .

I saw a dark and stormy ocean.

Over it the black clouds hung heavily; through them every now and then vivid lightning's flashed, and loud thunders rolled, while the winds moaned, and the waves rose and foamed, and fretted and broke, and rose to foam and fret and break again.

In that ocean I thought I saw myriads of poor human beings plunging and floating, and shouting and shrieking, and cursing and struggling, and drowning; and as they cursed and shrieked, they rose and shrieked again, and then sank to rise no more.

And out of this dark angry ocean I saw a mighty rock that rose up with its summit towering high above the black clouds that overhung the stormy sea; and all round the base of this rock I saw a vast platform; and on to this platform I saw with delight a number of the poor, struggling, drowning wretches continually climbing out of the angry ocean; and I saw that a number of those who were already safe on the platform were helping the poor creatures still in the angry waters to reach the same place of safety.

On looking more closely I found a number of those who had been rescued scheming and contriving by ladders and ropes and boats and other expedients more effectually to deliver the poor strugglers out of this sea.

Here and there were some who actually jumped into the water, regardless of all consequences, in their eagerness to "rescue the perishing;" and I hardly know which gladdened me most the sight of the poor people climbing on to the rocks, and so reaching the place of safety, or the devotion and self-sacrifice of those whose whole being was wrapped up in efforts for their deliverance...

. . . but only a very few of them seemed to make it their business to get the people out of the sea.

And as I looked I saw that the occupants of that platform were quite a mixed company. That is, they were divided into different "sets" or castes, and occupied themselves with different pleasures and employments; but only a very few of them seemed to make it their business to get the people out of the sea.

But what puzzled me most was the fact that though all had been rescued at one time or another from the ocean, nearly everyone seemed to have forgotten all about it.

Anyway, the memory of its darkness and danger no longer troubled them.

Then what was equally strange and perplexing to me was that these people did not seem to have any care—that is, any agonizing care—about the poor perishing ones who were struggling and drowning before their eyes, many of whom were their own husbands and wives, mothers and sisters and children.

And this unconcern could not have been the result of ignorance, because they lived right in sight of it all, and talked about it sometimes, and regularly went to hear lectures in which the awful state of the poor drowning creatures was described.

I have already said that the occupants of this platform were engaged in different pursuits. Some of them were absorbed night and day in trading, in order to make gain, storing up their savings in boxes, strong rooms, and the like.

. . . these people did not seem to have any care—that is, any agonizing care—about the poor perishing ones . . .

Many spent their time in amusing themselves with growing flowers on the side of the rock; others in painting pieces of cloth, or in playing music, or in dressing themselves up in different styles, and walking about to be admired. Some occupied themselves chiefly in eating and drinking, others were greatly taken up with arguing about the poor drowning creatures in the sea, and as to what would become of them in the future, while many contented themselves that they did their duty to the perishing creatures by the performance of curious religious ceremonies.

On looking more closely I found that some of the crowd who had reached the place of safety had discovered a passage up the rock leading to a higher platform still, which was fairly above the black clouds that overhung the ocean, and from which they had a good view of the mainland not very far away, and to which they expected to be taken off at some distant day. Here they passed their time in pleasant thoughts, congratulating themselves and one another on their good fortune in being rescued from the stormy deep, and singing songs about the happiness that would be theirs when they should be taken to the mainland.

A few others did much the same thing at times, working hard in their way; but the people who chiefly attracted my attention were at the business all the year round; indeed, they made such a terrible to-do about it, and went at it with such fierceness and fury, that many even of those who were doing the same kind of work, only in a milder way, were quite angry with them, and called them mad.

And then I saw something more wonderful still... The miseries and agonies, and perils and blasphemies, of these poor struggling people in this dark sea moved the pity of the great God in Heaven; moved it so much that He sent a Great Being to deliver them. And I thought that this Great Being whom Jehovah sent came straight from His palace, right through the black clouds, and leaped right into the raging sea among the drowning, sinking people; and there I saw Him toiling to rescue them, with tears and cries, until the sweat of His great anguish ran down in blood. And as He toiled and embraced the poor wretches, and tried to lift them on to the rock, He was continually crying to those already rescued— to those whom He had helped up with His own bleeding hands—to come and help Him in the painful and laborious task of saving their fellows.

And what seemed to me most passing strange was that those on the platform to whom He called, who heard His voice, and felt they ought to obey it—at least, they said they did—those who loved Him much, and were in

full sympathy with Him in the task He had undertaken—
who worshipped Him, or who professed to do so—were
so taken up with their trades and professions, and money
saving and pleasures, and families and circles, and religions
and arguments about it, and preparations for going to the
mainland, that they did not attend to the cry that came to
them from this wonderful Being who had Himself gone
down into the sea.

Anyway, if they heard it they did not heed it; they did not care; and so the multitude went on struggling, and shrieking, and drowning in the darkness.

Anyway, if they heard it they did not heed it; they did not care . . .

And then I saw something that seemed to me stranger than anything that had gone before in this strange vision.

I saw that some of these people on the platform, whom
this wonderful Being wanted to come and help Him in His
difficult task, were always praying and crying to Him to
come to them.

Some wanted Him to come and stay with them, and
spend His time and strength in making them happier.
Others wanted Him to come and take away various doubts
and misgivings they had respecting the truth of some letters
which He had written them.

Some wanted Him to come and make them feel more
secure on the rock—so secure that they would be quite sure
they should never slip off again. Numbers of others wanted
Him to make them feel quite certain that they would really
get on to the mainland some day; because, as a matter of

fact, it was well known that some had walked so carelessly as to miss their footing, and had fallen back again into the stormy waters.

So these people used to meet, and get as high up the rock as they could; and, looking towards the mainland, where they thought the Great Being was, they would cry out, "Come to us! Come, and help us!"

That sea was the ocean of life—the sea of real, actual human existence.

And all this time He was down among the poor struggling, drowning creatures in the angry deep, with His arms around them, trying to drag them out, and looking up—oh! so longingly, but all in vain-to those on the rock, crying to them, with His voice all hoarse with calling, "Come to me! COME, AND HELP ME!"

And then I understood it all. It was plain enough. That sea was the ocean of life—the sea of real, actual, human existence. That lightning was the gleaming of piercing truth coming from Jehovah's Throne. That thunder was the distant echoing of the wrath of God.

Those multitudes of people shrieking, struggling, agonizing in the stormy sea, were the thousands and thousands of poor harlots and harlot-makers, of drunkards and drunkard-makers, of thieves and liars, and blasphemers and ungodly people of every kindred, and tongue, and nation.

Oh, what a black sea it was! And oh, what multitudes of rich and poor, ignorant and educated were there, and all so unlike in their outward circumstances and conditions, yet all alike in one thing—all sinners before God; all held by, and holding on to, some iniquity, fascinated by some idol, the slaves of some devilish lust, and ruled by some foul fiend from the bottomless pit!

"All alike in one thing?" Nay, in two things—not only the same in their wickedness, but, unless rescued, alike in their sinking, sinking, sinking, down, down, down to the same terrible doom.

That great sheltering rock represented Calvary; and the people on it were those who had been rescued; and the way they employed their energies and gifts and time represented the occupations and amusements of those who profess to be rescued from sin and hell, and to be the followers of Jesus Christ. The handful of fierce, determined saviors were Salvation Soldiers, together with a few others who shared the same spirit. That mighty Being was the Son of God, "the same yesterday, and today, and for ever," who is still struggling to save the dying multitudes about us from this terrible doom of damnation, and whose voice can be heard, above the music, and machinery, and hue-and-cry of life, calling on the rescued to come and help Him to save the world.

My comrades, you are rescued from the waters; you are on the rock. He is in the dark sea, calling on you to come to Him and help Him. Will you go?

Look for yourselves. The surging sea of life crowded with perishing souls rolls up to the very spot on which you stand. Leaving the vision, I now come to speak of the fact— fact that is real as the Bible; as real as the Christ who hung upon the cross! as real as the Judgment Day will be, and as real as the Heaven and Hell that will follow it.

Look! Don't be deluded by appearances—men and things are not what they seem. All who are not on the rock are in the sea. Look at them from the standpoint of the Great White Throne, and what a sight you have!

Jesus Christ, the Son of God; is in the midst of this dying multitude, struggling to save them. And He is calling on YOU to jump into the sea—to go right away to His side, and help Him in the holy strife.

Will you jump? That is, will you go to His feet, and place yourself absolutely at His disposal?

Will you jump? That is, will you go to His feet, and place yourself entirely at His disposal?

A Soldier came to me once, saying that for some time she had been giving her Lord her profession, and prayers, and money, and now she wanted to give Him her body. She wanted to go right into the fight. In other words, she wanted to go to His assistance in the sea.

As when a man from the bank seeing another struggling in the water, lays aside those outer garments that would hinder his efforts, and leaps to the rescue, so will you who still linger on the bank, thinking, and singing, and praying about the poor perishing souls, lay aside your shame, your pride, your care about other people's opinions, your love of ease and all the selfish loves that have hindered you so long, and rush to the rescue of this multitude of dying men.

Does the surging sea look dark and dangerous? Unquestionably it is so. There is no doubt that the leap for you, as for every one who takes it, means difficulty, and scorn, and suffering. For you it may mean more than this. It may mean death. He who calls to you from the sea, however, knows what it will mean; and knowing, He still beckons you, and bids you come.

You must do it. You cannot hold back.

You have enjoyed yourself in religion long enough. You have had pleasant feelings, pleasant songs, pleasant meetings, pleasant prospects. There has been much of human happiness, much clapping of hands, and firing of volleys—very much of Heaven on earth.

Now, then, go to God, and tell Him you are prepared as far as necessary to turn your back upon it all, and that you are willing to spend the rest of your days grappling with these perishing multitudes, cost you what it may. You MUST do it.

With the light that has now broken in upon your mind, and the call that is now sounding in your ears, and the beckoning finger that is now before your eyes, you have no alternative. To go down among the perishing crowds is your duty. Your happiness henceforth will consist in sharing their misery; your ease in sharing their pain; your crown in bearing their cross; and your heaven in going to the very jaws of hell to rescue them.

WHAT WILL YOU DO?

An Introduction to The Fishless Fisherman:

> "Launch out into the deep, and let down
> your nets for a catch." and Jesus said . . .
> "From now on you will be fishers of men."
>
> —Luke 5:4,11

The Fishless Fisherman is a missions parable about being a "fisher of men." Many of us can recall singing the children's chorus, "I will make you fishers of men"; yet how many of us have applied this calling into our lives (to share the Gospel with the lost and to lead people to faith in Jesus Christ)?

This classic parable by John M. Drescher is hard-hitting and challenging. The parable is written as a satire, which means it uses "sarcasm or ridicule in the exposure of wrongful actions or attitudes." The story intentionally exaggerates the truth in order to prove a point, which in this case is the vital importance of sharing the Gospel of Jesus Christ with people who do not know Him.

As you read this parable, be assured that we deeply respect the importance and role of the local church and the calling of pastors. We also realize that Cod does not call every believer to full-time missionary work in foreign countries. Even so, every Christian is called to share the Gospel.

John M. Drescher:

For over 50 years, John M. Drescher has served in ministry as a pastor and overseer in the Mennonite Church. He is an author of 37 books, and a speaker on marriage and family life.

The Fishless Fisherman
A Mission Parable, by John M. Drescher

Now it came to pass that a group existed who called themselves fishermen. And lo, there were many fish in the waters all around. In fact, the whole area was surrounded by streams and lakes filled with fish.

And the fish were hungry.

Year after year these who called themselves fishermen met in meetings and talked about their call to fish, the abundance of fish, and how they might go about fishing.

Continually, they searched for new and better definitions of fishing. They sponsored costly nationwide and worldwide congresses to discuss fishing and promote fishing and hear about all the ways of fishing.

These fishermen built large, beautiful building called "Fishing Headquarters." The plea was that everyone should be a fisherman and every fisherman should fish. One thing they didn't do, however; they didn't fish.

They organized a board to send out fishermen to other places where there were many fish. The board was formed by those who had the great vision and courage

One thing they didn't do, however; they didn't fish.

to speak about fishing, to define fishing, and to promote the idea of fishing in far away streams and lakes where many other fish of different colors lived.

Also the board hired staffs and appointed committees and held many meetings to define fishing, to defend fishing, and to decide what new streams should be thought about. But the staff and committee members did not fish.

Expensive training centers were built to teach fishermen how to fish. Those who taught had doctorates in Fishology, but the teachers did not fish. They only taught fishing. Year after year, graduates were sent to do full-time fishing, some to distant waters filled with fish.

Further, the fishermen built large printing houses to publish fishing guides.

A speaker's bureau was also provided to schedule special speakers on the subject of fishing. Many who felt the call to be fishermen responded, and were sent to fish. But like the fishermen back home, they never fished.

Some also said they wanted to be a part of the fishing party, but they felt called to furnish fishing equipment. Others felt their job was to relate to the fish in a good way so the fish would know the difference between good and bad fishermen.

After one stirring meeting on "The Necessity for Fishing," a young fellow left the meeting and went fishing. The next day he reported he had caught two outstanding fish.

He was honored for his excellent catch and scheduled to visit all the big meetings possible to tell how he did it. So he quit fishing in order to have time to tell about the experience to the other fishermen.

He was also placed on the Fishermen's General Board as a person having considerable experience.

Now it's true that many of the fishermen sacrificed and put up with all kinds of difficulties.

Some lived near the water and bore the smell of dead fish every day. They received the ridicule of some who made fun of their fishermen's clubs and the fact that they claimed to be fishermen yet never fished. They wondered about those who felt it was of little use to attend the weekly meetings to talk about fishing.

After all, were they not following the Master who said, "Follow me, and I will make you fishers of men?"

After all, were they not following the Master who said, "Follow me, and I will make you fishers of men?"

Imagine how hurt some were when one day a person suggested that those who didn't catch fish were really not fishermen, no matter how much they claimed to be. Yet it did sound correct.

Is a person a fisherman if year after year he never catches a fish?

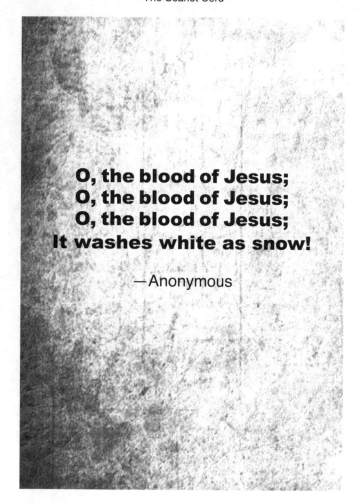

O, the blood of Jesus;
O, the blood of Jesus;
O, the blood of Jesus;
It washes white as snow!

—Anonymous

11

Remembering the Blood

Communion Verses and Hymns

As Christians, when we partake of the bread and the cup during a communion service, we are remembering the sacrifice of our Lord on the cross.

Jesus said, "Do this in remembrance of Me."

When we partake of communion, the elements do not literally become Jesus' broken body and His shed blood—sacrificed over and over again—as if our Lord's final sacrifice was not enough. Instead, the bread and the cup are symbolic of God's finished work of salvation—they are symbols of our Passover lamb and God's scarlet cord—offered once and for all on the cross of Calvary. We remember Christ's words on the cross as He paid the ultimate and final sacrifice. Jesus said, "It is finished."

The bread reminds us of Christ's body which was broken for us, and the cup reminds us of Christ's blood which was shed for our forgiveness. As we partake of communion—either corporately in a church service or in the privacy of our own homes (with our family, our spouse, fellow believers, or alone with the Lord)—we remember all that God has done for us and for the world. We remember His body and blood, and our salvation.

Taking the bread . . .

1 Corinthians 11:23-24

For I received from the Lord that which I also
delivered to you: that the Lord Jesus on the same
night in which He was betrayed took bread; and
when He had given thanks, He broke it and said,
"Take, eat; this is My body which is broken for you;
do this in remembrance of Me."

1 Peter 2:24

Who Himself bore our sins in His own body on
the tree, that we, having died to sins, might live for
righteousness—by whose stripes you were healed.

Taking the cup . . .

1 Corinthians 11:25-29

In the same manner He also took the cup after supper,
saying, "This cup is the new covenant in My blood.
This do, as often as you drink it, in remembrance of
Me."

For as often as you eat this bread and drink this
cup, you proclaim the Lord's death till He comes.
Therefore whoever eats this bread or drinks this cup
of the Lord in an unworthy manner will be guilty of
the body and blood of the Lord.

But let a man examine himself, and so let him eat of
the bread and drink of the cup.

For he who eats and drinks in an unworthy manner
eats and drinks judgment to himself, not discerning
the Lord's body.

More Communion Verses:

Isaiah 1:18

. . . though your sins are like scarlet, they shall be as white as snow.

Matthew 26:1-2, 26-28

Now it came to pass, when Jesus had finished all these sayings, that He said to His disciples, "You know that after two days is the Passover, and the Son of Man will be delivered up to be crucified." And as they were eating, Jesus took bread, blessed and broke it, and gave it to the disciples and said, "Take, eat; this is My body."

Then He took the cup, and gave thanks, and gave it to them, saying, "Drink from it, all of you. For this is My blood of the new covenant, which is shed for many for the remission of sins.

Mark 14:22-25

And as they were eating, Jesus took bread, blessed and broke it, and gave it to them and said, "Take, eat; this is My body."

Then He took the cup, and when He had given thanks He gave it to them, and they all drank from it. And He said to them, "This is My blood of the new covenant, which is shed for many.

Assuredly, I say to you, I will no longer drink of the fruit of the vine until that day when I drink it new in the kingdom of God."

Luke 22:14-20

When the hour had come, He sat down, and the twelve apostles with Him. Then He said to them, "With fervent desire I have desired to eat this Passover with you before I suffer; for I say to you,

I will no longer eat of it until it is fulfilled in the kingdom of God."

Then He took the cup, and gave thanks, and said, "Take this and divide it among yourselves; for I say to you, I will not drink of the fruit of the vine until the kingdom of God comes." And He took bread, gave thanks and broke it, and gave it to them, saying, "This is My body which is given for you; do this in remembrance of Me." Likewise He also took the cup after supper, saying, "This cup is the new covenant in My blood, which is shed for you.

1 Corinthians 5:7

Therefore purge out the old leaven, that you may be a new lump, since you truly are unleavened. For indeed Christ, our Passover, was sacrificed for us.

1 Corinthians 10:16

The cup of blessing which we bless, is it not the communion of the blood of Christ? The bread which we break, is it not the communion of the body of Christ?

1 John 1:7

...the blood of Jesus Christ His Son cleanses us from all sin.

Acts 2:42

And they continued steadfastly in the apostles' doctrine and fellowship, in the breaking of bread, and in prayers.

John 6:48-58

I am the bread of life. Your fathers ate the manna in the wilderness, and are dead. This is the bread which comes down from heaven, that one may eat of it and not die. I am the living bread which came down from heaven. If anyone eats of this bread, he will live forever; and the bread that I shall give is My flesh, which I shall give for the life of the world."

The Jews therefore quarreled among themselves, saying, "How can this Man give us His flesh to eat?"

Then Jesus said to them, "Most assuredly, I say to you, unless you eat the flesh of the Son of Man and drink His blood, you have no life in you.

Whoever eats My flesh and drinks My blood has eternal life, and I will raise him up at the last day. For My flesh is food indeed, and My blood is drink indeed.

He who eats My flesh and drinks My blood abides in Me, and I in him. As the living Father sent Me, and I live because of the Father, so he who feeds on Me will live because of Me. This is the bread which came down from heaven—not as your fathers ate the manna, and are dead. He who eats this bread will live forever."

Hebrews 13:8
Jesus Christ, the same, yesterday, today, and forever.

Revelation 13:8
. . . the Lamb slain from the foundation of the world.

Communion Hymns

Nothing but the Blood
—Hymn lyrics and music by Robert Lowry

What can wash away my sin?
Nothing but the blood of Jesus;
What can make me whole again?
Nothing but the blood of Jesus.

Oh! precious is the flow
That makes me white as snow;
No other fount I know,
Nothing but the blood of Jesus.

For my pardon, this I see,
Nothing but the blood of Jesus;
For my cleansing this my plea,
Nothing but the blood of Jesus.

Nothing can for sin atone,
Nothing but the blood of Jesus;
Naught of good that I have done,
Nothing but the blood of Jesus.

This is all my hope and peace,
Nothing but the blood of Jesus;
This is all my righteousness,
Nothing but the blood of Jesus.

Glory! Glory! This I sing
Nothing but the blood of Jesus;
All my praise for this I bring
Nothing but the blood of Jesus.

Just as I Am
—Hymn lyrics by Charlotte Elliot
—Music by William B. Bradbury

Just as I am, without one plea,
But that Thy blood was shed for me,
And that Thou bidst me come to Thee,
O Lamb of God, I come, I come.

Just as I am, and waiting not
To rid my soul of one dark blot,
To Thee whose blood can cleanse each spot,
O Lamb of God, I come, I come.

Just as I am, Thou wilt receive,
Wilt welcome, pardon, cleanse, relieve;
Because Thy promise I believe,
O Lamb of God, I come, I come.

Just as I am, Thy love unknown
Hath broken every barrier down;
Now, to be Thine, yea, Thine alone,
O Lamb of God, I come, I come.

Just as I am, of that free love
The breadth, length, depth, and height to prove,
Here for a season, then above,
O Lamb of God, I come, I come!

Tis so Sweet to Trust in Jesus
—Hymn lyrics by Louisa M. R. Stead,
—Music by William J. Kirkpatrick

'Tis so sweet to trust in Jesus,
Just to take Him at His Word;
Just to rest upon His promise,
Just to know, "Thus says the Lord!"

Jesus, Jesus, how I trust Him!
How I've proved Him o'er and o'er!
Jesus, Jesus, precious Jesus!
O for grace to trust Him more!

O how sweet to trust in Jesus,
Just to trust His cleansing blood;
Just in simple faith to plunge me
'Neath the healing, cleansing flood!

Yes, 'tis sweet to trust in Jesus,
Just from sin and self to cease;
Just from Jesus simply taking
Life and rest, and joy and peace.

I'm so glad I learned to trust Thee,
Precious Jesus, Savior, Friend;
And I know that Thou art with me,
Wilt be with me to the end.

O For a Thousand Tongues to Sing
—Hymn lyrics by Charles Wesley

O for a thousand tongues to sing
My great Redeemer's praise,
The glories of my God and King,
The triumphs of His grace!

My gracious Master and my God,
Assist me to proclaim,
To spread through all the earth abroad
The honors of Thy name.

Jesus! the name that charms our fears,
That bids our sorrows cease;
'Tis music in the sinner's ears,
'Tis life, and health, and peace.

He breaks the power of canceled sin,
He sets the prisoner free;
His blood can make the foulest clean,
His blood availed for me.

The Blood Will Never Lose Its Power
—From the lyrics & music by Andre Crouch

It reaches to the highest mountain,
It flows to the lowest valley,
The blood that gives me strength
From day to day,
It will never lose its power.

There's Power in Blood
—Hymn lyrics & music: Lewis E. Jones, 1899

Would you be free from the burden of sin?
There's power in the blood, power in the blood;
Would you o'er evil a victory win?

There's wonderful power in the blood.

There is power, power, wonder working power
In the blood of the Lamb;
There is power, power, wonder working power
In the precious blood of the Lamb.

Would you be free from your passion and pride?
There's power in the blood, power in the blood;
Come for a cleansing to Calvary's tide;
There's wonderful power in the blood.

Would you be whiter, much whiter than snow?
There's power in the blood, power in the blood;
Sin stains are lost in its life giving flow.
There's wonderful power in the blood.

Would you do service for Jesus your King? There's
power in the blood, power in the blood;
Would you live daily His praises to sing?
There's wonderful power in the blood.

Often, as the elements of
Communion are served, a minister will
ask the congregation,

"Has everyone been served?"

As disciples of Jesus Christ,
let us remember the multitudes
all throughout the world,
who are still waiting to be served.

May God compell us
to GO to them with the Gospel.

**On the cross,
Jesus bled out completely—
He held nothing back!
In return,
God wants you to give
everything to Him—
to hold nothing back!**

—Jon Dunagan

One Final Word

If you have never completely and whole-heartedly surrendered your life to the Lord Jesus Christ, and put your complete trust in His precious blood-offered for YOU, on the cross of Calvary-to forgive you of your sins and to save you, we invite you to call out to God, right now, for His mercy, grace, and salvation.

The Bible says:

> "For the wages of sin is death,
> but the gift of God is eternal life
> through Jesus Christ our Lord."
> —Romans 6:23

> "If you confess with your mouth the Lord Jesus,
> and believe in your heart that God has
> raised Him from the dead, you shall be saved."
> —Romans 10:9

> "For 'whoever calls on the name of
> the LORD shall be saved.'"
> —Romans 10:13

> "Behold, now is the accepted time;
> behold, now is the day of salvation."
> —II Corinthians 6:2

An example of a prayer, asking for God's salvation:

Dear Lord God, I repent of my sins, and ask You to forgive me and to cleanse me through the perfect blood of Your Son, Jesus Christ. I believe Jesus died on the cross for my sins, and that He rose from the dead. I surrender entirely to You, and submit to Your call and purposes for my life. I love You, Lord, and entrust my whole life completely to You, forever. -In Jesus" Name, Amen.

**Oh, precious is the flow!
That makes me white as snow.
No other fount I know.
Nothing but the blood
of Jesus!**

—Robert Lowry

Notes:

Preface:

"A Passion for Souls" -Hebert G. Tovey, 1888. Words of this
hymn are in public domain.

Chapter 1.

Radical, by David Platt (Multnomah Books, 2010), pp. 143.

Erasing Hell, by Francis Chan and Preston Sprinkle (David
C. Cook, 2011), pp. 147, 148. (In direct response to *Love
Wins*, by Rob Bell, *Erasing Hell* addresses the biblical
reality of hell.)

Chapters 2, 3, 4, 7.

Mission statistics compiled from *World Christian
Encyclopedia*, edited by David B. Barrett, George T.
Kurian, and Todd M. Johnson (Oxford University
Press, 2001); *Revolution in World Missions*, by K.P.
Yohannan (Gospel for Asia), and a brochure, *The
Glaring Injustice of 21st Century Missions* (www.
missionindia.org).

Biblical and theological statistics for "The Great Commission
and Great Confusion" are from *The Dake Annotated
Reference Bible* (Dake Publishing), commentary notes
by Mark 16.

10 Reasons to Pray for the Lost, Special thanks to Pastor
Dee Duke, from a message given at Christian Renewal
Center.

Chapter 8.

Missionary and martyr statistics and dates were verified
on Wikipedia (2011), and from various online
documentation.

"Dr. Duff's Appeal" by Oswald J. Smith, from *The Challenge of Missions* (Waynesboro, GA): Operation Mobilization, 1959), pp. 37-38. (This book is out of print but was reprinted in 2003 by Eternal Word Ministries.) Used by permission of People's Church, Toronto, Canada, and the family of Oswald J. Smith.

"The Man in the Clouds" by Paul Eshleman, director of the Jesus Film Project (from a missions letter). Used with permission.

Chapter 9.

"Thy Brother's Blood Crieth," by Amy Carmichal. Published by the Dohnavur Fellowship. Public domain.

"The Whole Estate," by Oswald J. Smith, from *The Challenge of Missions*. Used with permission.

"Who Cares?" by General William Booth, The Salvation Army. Public domain (also used with permission).

"The Fishless Fisherman," by John M. Drescher. Used with permission from the author.

Chapter 10.

Lyrics for all of the featured hymns about the blood of Jesus are in public domain.

About the Authors:

Jon Dunagan is an international evangelist, focused on preaching the Good News of Jesus Christ. Proclaiming the Gospel to crowds of thousands and to individuals one-on-one, Jon has ministered on all seven continents. Along with world missions, Jon enjoys prayer walks, tropical snorkeling, African wildlife safaris, fishing, and time with his family.

Ann Dunagan is a homeschooling mother, co-founder of Harvest Ministry's orphan outreach (caring for over 1000 children) and podcaster at *Mission-Minded Families* (featured on many radio broadcasts, including Revive Our Hearts and Family Life Today). Ann ministers internationally alongside her husband Jon; and through her books, teaching curriculum, and online writing, she motivates families for world missions.

Jon & Ann Dunagan have seven children, and collectively, they and their mission-minded family have traveled and ministered in over 100 nations.

About Harvest Ministry:

Harvest Ministry is a Christian evangelistic outreach, founded in 1987 by Jon & Ann Dunagan with the primary purpose of reaching the lost for Jesus Christ (reaping a "harvest" of souls for God's Kingdom), especially in remote areas where the Gospel has not yet been publicly proclaimed. Specific mission focus areas include winning souls, loving orphans, serving churches, equipping national ministers, and motivating mission-minded families.

Mission-Minded Resources:

For more books by the Dunagans see
http://missionmindedfamilies.org

Please see Harvest Ministry's website for many FREE mission-minded resources for families.

For information about ordering additional copies of *The Scarlet Cord: Nothing but the Blood of Jesus* (including bulk orders for church or ministry distribution) please contact:

HarvestMinistry.org
MissionMindedFamilies.org

Revelation 12:11

And they overcame him
by the blood of the lamb, and
by the word of their testimony,
and they loved not their lives
unto the death.